Performance Appraisal on the Line

Performance Appraisal on the Line

DAVID L. DEVRIES
ANN M. MORRISON
SANDRA L. SHULLMAN
MICHAEL L. GERLACH

A CENTER FOR CREATIVE LEADERSHIP
PUBLICATION
Greensboro, North Carolina

This publication is designed to provide accurate and authoritative information in regard to the subject matter covered. It is sold with the understanding that the publisher is not engaged in rendering legal, accounting, or other professional service. If legal advice or other expert assistance is required, the services of a competent professional person should be sought. *From a Declaration of Principles jointly adopted by a Committee of the American Bar Association and a Committee of Publishers.*

Library of Congress Cataloging in Publication Data:

Main entry under title:

Performance appraisal on the line.

"A Center For Creative Leadership Publication"
Bibliography: p.
Includes indexes.
1. Employees, Rating of. I. DeVries, David L.
HF5549.5.R3P46 658.3′125 81-10328
ISBN-0-912879-93-9 AACR2

Printed in the United States of America

10 9 8 7 6 5 4 3 2

Preface

**I write first of all for myself.
That is how I learn.**

This sentiment of Henry Mintzberg captures our reasons for writing this book. The individual and collective work we have done with performance appraisal (PA) has brought us into contact with many human resource professionals. Through interviews, workshops, and casual conversations we have mulled over many issues related to appraising employees. In this book we have attempted to put these insights to a tough test: to combine them into a perspective useful to practitioners, which does not ignore the reality of our very limited grasp on this complex phenomenon.

How we wrote this manuscript may be as significant as the topic we chose. Any manuscript coauthored by four professionals is by itself an interesting phenomenon. Although the frustrations of such collaboration may seem most obvious (endless debates, varying writing styles, and scheduling problems), the assets are also present. Because the authors come with diverse professional perspectives, the full complexity of PA (as an organizational intervention, feedback process, and exercise in judgment) was matched by our interests. The team also had an excellent object lesson in resolving conflicts among professionals, each of whose positions had merit. Such controversy is not to be skirted but rather encouraged. The PA literature should more directly embody such controversy.

The number of behind-the-scenes contributors to a manuscript of this sort is always amazing. The staff of the Center for Creative Leadership, Greensboro, North Carolina, provides authors with truly professional guidance. We are grateful to several people for their significant contributions to this manuscript. Mary Ellen Kranz contributed ideas, feedback, and research assistance throughout the writing and revision stages, and she helped make this book an exciting venture. The suggestions of Morgan McCall and Charles Hansen were also valuable in drafting and revising the manuscript. Jane Swanson managed the complex process of typing, revising, proofing, and otherwise producing this manuscript in a professional and dedicated manner. Mildred Dohm and Alice Warren typed the manuscript with patience and a sense of order not always warranted by the input from the authors.

Norma Kay compiled, organized, and referenced much of the literature in the review process. Frank Freeman and Karen Barden also proved to be dedicated detectives in accessing key articles in a literature which spans many journals. Crystal Burnette and Vickie Straughan assisted in preparing the final manuscript, and Joanne Ferguson did the final proofing.

Many other staff members also supported this effort, particularly those who served as professional reviewers. We also received valuable reviews from Edward Lawler and Nathan Winstanley.

This review was originally prepared as part of a larger project funded by the General Electric Company and directed by Selig M. Danzig on the Corporate Employee Relations staff. We are grateful to Selig and other managers at General Electric who gave their support to this work.

Greensboro, North Carolina
June 1981

David L. DeVries
Ann M. Morrison
Sandra L. Shullman
Michael L. Gerlach

Contents

CHAPTER 3

CHAPTER 4

CHAPTER 5

CHAPTER 8

Performance Appraisal on the Line

1

An Overview of Performance Appraisal and the Literature

Item: As a division manager, you are faced with a deteriorating profit situation caused by increasing costs of manufacturing, marketing, and distributing your products. You have set the goal of reducing costs across-the-board by at least 5%. You need a way to translate this goal into concrete actions for each of your employees.

Item: You are a chief executive officer (CEO) of a medium-sized manufacturing company. You have always prided yourself on paying competitively and allowing your managers to decide how to divvy up the pool of new salary money. Now that double-digit inflation has arrived, you are hearing more complaints about the fairness of the system. Most troublesome is that some of your star performers are telling you that several managers are giving all employees the same percentage salary increase. You need a way for your managers to decide who is doing well and not so well so that the salary pie can be sliced up according to performance.

Item: A female accountant was recently terminated by one of your managers. The woman's lawyer has notified you that a class-action suit alleging discriminatory treatment has been filed. Your former employee alleges being summarily fired, whereas your manager says she was always a marginal employee. When you check with your manager, you find out that at no point during her tenure was the former accountant informed of this. You desperately want to avoid this situation in the future.

These items are challenges shared with us in interviews by managers and professionals from several corporations. What ties them together is the common solution they proposed to all these management dilemmas. That solution is performance appraisal (PA)—the basic, yet baffling, process of determining how an individual employee is performing.

The importance of PA is suggested by the wide range of managerial dilemmas for which it is held accountable.

This review focuses on PA as a management tool using and supplementing the formal literature to assess how PA was used in the past, how PA is used now, and the direction PA is likely to take in the future. This chapter provides some background on PA and summarizes what the review involved, why we did the review, and what you can expect from the review.

WHAT IS PERFORMANCE APPRAISAL?

How is PA defined? One way is to cite what the experts in the literature suggest should be happening under the guise of PA. Another way is to describe the basic cognitive and interpersonal processes underlying this complex phenomenon. We chose a third alternative. The definition we use flows from how organizations currently do PA.

Performance appraisal is, in short, the process by which an organization measures and evaluates an individual employee's behavior and accomplishments for a finite time period. Evaluations are typically done annually by the employee's immediate manager. The judgments are often subsequently used to make administrative decisions (e.g., for salary or promotion) that directly affect the employee.

The cycle of events that constitutes PA can be examined from two levels: *(a)* the organization in which the issues of maintaining the PA system and using appraisal data are relevant and *(b)* the manager–employee pair directly involved in the appraisal.

PA from an Organizational Perspective

The PA process for organizations is typically led by the personnel function during the tenth through twelfth month of an annual period. Personnel offices often view PA as a six-step sequence, of the sort outlined in Figure 1. The sequence is significant because it begins and ends with the personnel function and is ultimately justified by the value of PA in helping make several administrative decisions.

PA from a Manager's Viewpoint

Understanding how a manager experiences PA is important because so much of the responsibility for doing PA lies directly on the manager's

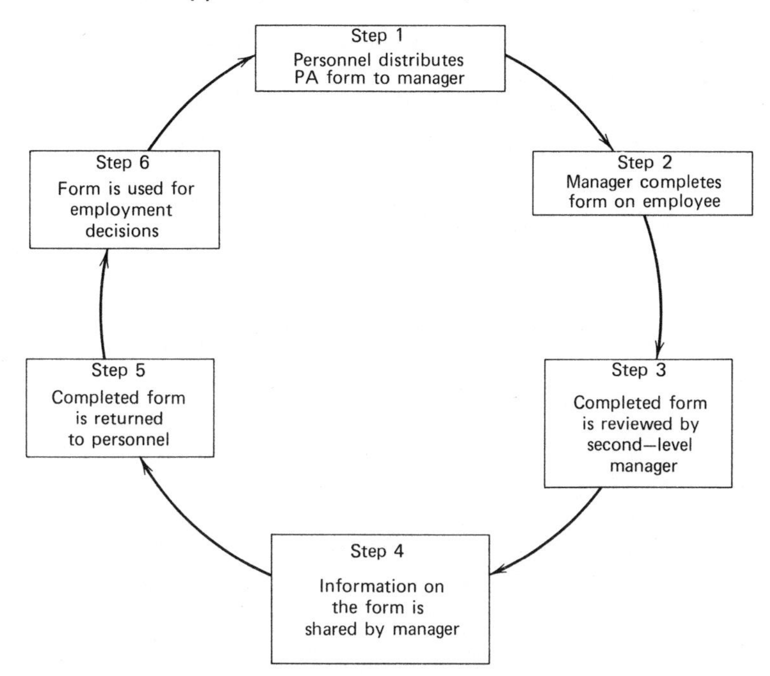

Figure 1 The PA scenario as an organizational event.

shoulder. As Exhibit 1 indicates, the manager is usually asked to go through a different six-step sequence that is at least theoretically spread throughout the entire year. The manager is asked to define the demands of the employee's position and translate these into some expectations for the employee, such as "I expect you to reduce absenteeism by 20%" or "I expect you to respond promptly to customers' requests for service." How the employee actually performs is observed by the manager over much of the 12-month period, resulting in a final evaluation that is documented on a form. These evaluations are shared with the subordinate, typically in a face-to-face discussion. The process ends with recommendations from the manager to higher management for one or more administrative decisions regarding the employee, decisions that the manager then announces to the employee.

PA is Many Things to Many People

Understanding what PA is requires recognition of its complexity. Consider, for example, the following:

1 PA simultaneously involves several interested parties—the employee, his/her manager, and the larger organization.

Exhibit 1 The PA Scenario: As a Managerial Tool

Step 1: Manager shares expectations for employee
⟶
Step 2: Manager observes/evaluates employee's performance
⟶
Step 3: Manager documents employee's performance
→
Step 4: Manager shares evaluation with employee
→
Step 5: Manager recommends administrative actions
→
Step 6: Manager announces administrative decisions
→

(12-month period)

2 PA goes far beyond simply filling out forms. It involves some difficult decisions by the manager about what is required of the employee and how the employee compares with these expectations, as well as constructive communication of these decisions with the subordinate.
3 PA is the centerpiece of human resource programs in many organizations. PA is often a basic building block for other programs, such as salary administration. Also, PA is often the only formal system organizations use to communicate to the employee what his/her job is.

WHAT ARE THE CRITICAL PA ISSUES?

There are two distinct audiences trying to understand more about PA. One audience consists of practitioners, often human resource professionals, who are charged with designing, implementing, and evaluating PA in their organization and who have an immediate, widespread impact on how PA is actually done by managers. A second audience consists of the knowledge generators, or researchers, who are pushing PA into new directions and who document the effectiveness of new PA variations.

Each audience helps define the current status and future of PA, yet each confronts a different set of issues around PA.

Issues for Practitioners

Practitioners have a habit of asking basic and troublesome questions about PA. These questions fall into the five categories listed next. These five issues, as a whole, constitute the major policy and operational decisions that are made whenever PA systems are developed, changed, or even dropped.

1 What is the rationale for doing PA at all?
   a What purposes can or should PA serve (such as increasing employees' productivity, improving manager–employee relationships, or simply supporting other human resource programs like salary administration)?
   b Is the impact of PA worth the investment it requires (such as training managers to do PA well)?
2 What characterizes effective PA systems?
   a How is "effective" defined? Does effectiveness depend on specifying certain desired outcomes? Are some general approaches to PA more effective than others (such as management by objectives (MBO))?
   b Is there one best way to measure performance, or are different methods needed for different employee groups? Who should evaluate an employee's performance (such as the supervisor, peers, or subordinates)?
3 What is the role of PA in the larger personnel and management picture?
   a Should PA be the foundation for other human resource programs (such as salary administration, management development, and redundancy planning)?
   b What role does PA play in the overall managerial role (such as communication with employees or planning work flow)?
4 How should PA systems be designed and implemented in an organization?
   a How can an existing PA system be changed to better serve the current needs of an organization?
   b Is there a way to introduce a PA program that will get a more enthusiastic response from employees?
5 What kinds of factors will affect PA in the 1980s?
   a Will behavioral science research better explain the mysterious decision-making processes involved in PA?
   b How will PA programs be changed as a result of the changing U.S. work force, government regulation, or the increasing complexity of management jobs?

Issues for PA "Experts"

Having just listed a broad range of questions raised regularly by practitioners, we think that it is useful to compare these with topics of concern to professionals generating prescriptions for improving PA. These issues are taken from the PA literature of the past 20 years and represent areas in which significant original research has been done.

1 What is the impact of involving the employee being evaluated in PA? Is the employee more satisfied or more likely to perform better when encouraged to participate actively in PA?

2 Can a PA form be created to evaluate an employee on factors most relevant to doing the job well (and avoid rating managers on "personal appearance" or "keeps work area clean")? Can PA rating scales be made more specific and useful than the traditional "marginal" to "excellent" continuum?

3 How can PA be made more bottom-line oriented? Can objective, measurable criteria be designed so that it is clear whether an employee accomplished results important for the organization?

These three issues have been the playground for research on PA over the past two decades. The prominent themes have been subordinate participation, behaviorally based rating scales, MBO, and goal setting. These themes are explored in some depth in this review.

The primary lesson to be learned from the two lists of issues is that one is only a small subset of the other. The issues being tackled by PA researchers fall almost totally within the second issue in the practitioners' list (What characterizes effective PA systems?). The implications for this single-minded focus of the research are profound. The literature yields some useful prescriptions about how to do PA but offers little help in addressing the issues of purposes, strategies for forming PA systems, and the relationships of PA with other personnel systems. The point is not made to fault the research community but to explain why PA research seems so irrelevant to many practitioners.

STRUCTURE AND CONTENT OF THE REVIEW

This review of the PA literature is organized around the five critical issues faced by practitioners. However, because the literature is focused on only one of these five issues (what characterizes effective PA systems), not all five issues receive equal treatment. Although we do not avoid tackling such issues as "How can PA systems be effectively introduced into organizations?" the treatment is by necessity at a more general level and is based at least as much on the authors' experience as on the literature.

Exhibit 2 Structure of the Review

Past	Present	Future
Practices and purposes shared (Chapter 2)	Practices (Chapter 2)	Theoretical advances (Chapter 7)
	Core measurement process (Chapter 3)	Environmental forces (Chapter 8)
	Contextual factors, participants (Chapter 4)	
	Comparison of PA systems (Chapter 5)	
	Implementing PA (Chapter 6)	

Exhibit 2 shows how the review unfolds over the next seven chapters. The treatment of the literature we use focuses on the following.

Past Practices

A review of the origins and evolution of PA, describing both how and why PA was conducted in organizations (Chapter 2).

Present Practices

A summary of current PA practices (Chapter 2) and a detailed look at what dimensions of PA systems are critical, including measurement strategies (Chapter 3) and the role of the participants (Chapter 4). The section continues with a systematic comparison of the prominent PA alternatives available to organizations (Chapter 5) and concludes with a model for placing a PA system into an organization (Chapter 6).

Future Practices

A review of recent developments in the understanding we have of managerial behavior that are likely to change PA (Chapter 7) and a summary of how major forces in the organization (such as the changing work force) and society at large are likely to affect PA (Chapter 8).

Any time a group of "experts" makes proclamations, a careful scrutiny of the bases of their claims is in order. A description of the methods we used follows, including some of the decisions we had to make in writing this review.

Intended Audience

The primary audience consists of human resources professionals responsible for designing, implementing, and evaluating PA programs as part of a larger human resource program. Secondary audiences are fellow professionals actively conducting research in PA and line managers who have been assigned a decision-making or monitoring role for PA and other human resource programs.

Information Bases

The primary source of information was the formal literature. We reviewed over 200 articles and books dealing directly with PA. The review focuses on the past five years as an update to a prior review conducted by one of the authors. The emphasis is on *(a)* original research reporting some new and, we hope, believable results with PA and *(b)* recent reviews of specific PA topics.

A second set of sources built on work conducted by the Center for Creative Leadership staff over the past four years. This included PA workshops for over 300 human resource professionals, interviews on the subject with over 100 line managers, and survey data from over 1000 managers and professionals. The value of these activities in gaining new perspectives on this topic cannot be overestimated.

Limitations of the Review

Any literature review has blind spots. Some of the more obvious limitations of this review are these:

1 The review focuses only on PA literature, not related literatures. Only in Chapter 7 are literatures cited that cover some of the basic psychological processes (e.g., information processing) central to PA.
2 The work of the Center for Creative Leadership staff has focused on PA programs for managers and professionals, and this review also

concentrates on that population. Although the literature does not address the question, the authors recognize that PA for represented hourly employees probably involves different dynamics.

3 The review places only secondary importance on an approach to PA still prominent in the literature—developing psychometrically sophisticated instruments. Whereas this approach aims at one definition of validity, the authors have seen too many instances of such PA systems that, because of their complexity, become "invalidated" through spotty use by managers.

4 Much has been written about PA, and the review is not exhaustive in covering all articles published on any given PA issue. Whenever possible, we used a combination of original studies of special import and already-existing literature reviews in addressing each issue.

5 The review does not give the reader a guaranteed step-by-step approach to PA in a given organization. To promise that would be to violate the judgment we have of the current state of knowledge about PA. The review is intended to give the reader a sense of what questions should be asked about a PA system (existing or proposed) and some likely trade-offs encountered any time one of the more frequently mentioned PA strategies is selected.

IN CONCLUSION

This chapter has described the types of questions (from both the world of research and practice) tackled in this review. Some of the more substantive themes that run through the review are these:

1 PA is in a troubled state; it makes great theoretical sense but falters in actual practice.

2 What is expected of PA in an organization is as important as the actual PA methods used in determining how well PA works; organizational expectations for PA may be unrealistic and at times even conflicting.

3 PA, although an imperfect tool, is here to stay. It can serve key organizational needs, legal requirements, and even the employee's need to know where he/she stands.

4 Most of what we know about PA is how to do it; much less is known about why PA is done, when PA is done, and who does PA. The PA literature, because of its narrow focus, leaves practitioners fending for themselves with many issues.

We suggest that you read the review in order, from Chapter 2 through 8, since each chapter is designed to build on the prior ones. We hope that this review will give you the following:

1. A healthy respect for the complexity of PA.
2. Some concrete help with (and moral support for) tackling specific PA issues.
3. A sense of what roles PA can and should play in organizations, as well as those for which PA is clearly inappropriate.

2

The History and Current Status of Performance Appraisal

Behavioral science applications to organizations have mushroomed in the last 25 years, and PA has been at the forefront of this boom. Today, PA is an almost universally accepted fact of organizational life. The approaches to and reasons for PA have changed in some ways during this time; for example, MBO has emerged as a different approach to appraisal, and legal considerations have become increasingly important. But the basic PA scenarios as outlined in Chapter 1 have remained much the same.

One purpose of this chapter is to put PA into a historical context. Despite its current popularity, PA is not new, and many of the issues now being addressed are old ones. A historical look at PA will help highlight the alternatives that have been tried before and the philosophies behind different approaches to PA. Another purpose is to examine the current status of PA as a basis from which readers can compare their own PA programs. We examine the status of some specific technical issues around PA: the prevalence of PA in different organizations, the types of systems being used, the factors being rated, and the evidence of the extent and quality of PA use in actual practice within organizations.

This chapter also explores reasons for instituting formal appraisal programs—reasons both stated and unstated—to put PA into perspective as a management tool within a larger organizational context. Understanding what approaches to PA are currently being taken, the reasons for taking the approaches, and how the approaches evolved will provide background for understanding subsequent chapters.

PA IN HISTORICAL PERSPECTIVE

Exhibit 3 summarizes how PA methods and uses have evolved over the past 80 years. Two trends are particularly striking. The first is that although new

Exhibit 3 Historical Events and Trends in PA

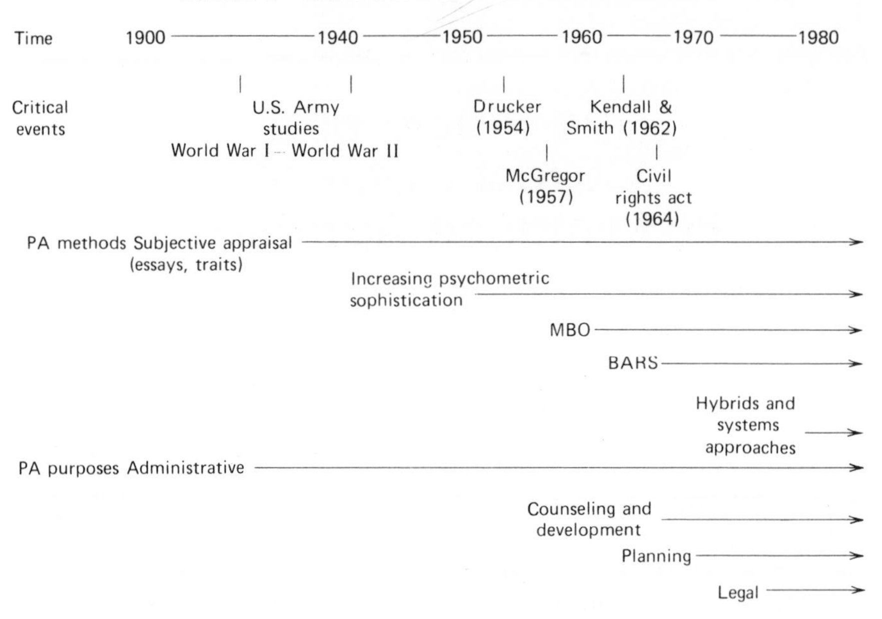

PA methods such as MBO and behaviorally anchored rating scales (BARS) have been adopted old methods such as essay forms and crude trait-rating scales are still prevalent. The "evolution" of PA has not entailed elimination of old methods in the face of the new.

The second striking trend shown in Exhibit 3 is that the purposes for PA have mushroomed over the past 20 years. PA systems are now being called on to serve far more functions than ever before, ranging from administrative use to employee development, corporate planning, and legal documentation.

A prominent theme of this review is that PA is being called on to do more than it is capable of delivering. This problem is compounded by two factors. One, although purposes for PA have expanded, many organizations continue to use PA methods developed decades ago when both the constraints on and uses for PA were minimal. Two, some purposes for PA are not necessarily compatible with other PA purposes. Several authors, for instance, have argued that asking managers to use PA to rate their employees so that this information can be used in salary and promotion decisions is incompatible with asking them to also use PA as a counseling and developmental tool for those same employees (classic articles exploring this point include Levinson, 1970; Meyer, Kay, & French, 1965). The recent emergence of PA as a tool for legal documentation will no doubt further compound this problem.

PA in Childhood

The widespread interest in PA systems over the last several decades should not obscure the fact that formal appraisal of employees has existed for centuries. As early as the third century A.D., emperors of the Wei dynasty employed an "Imperial Rater" to rate the performance of the official family members. The early criticism of this system by Chinese philosopher Sin Yu foreshadows criticism still heard about PA: "The Imperial Rater of Nine Grades seldom rates men according to their merits but always according to his likes and dislikes" (Patten, 1977, p. 352).

PA in industry was probably begun by Robert Owen in the early 1800s in his cotton mills of Scotland. Over each employee's work station hung a cube of wood denoting, according to shade from light to dark, the different grades of deportment—white for excellent, yellow for good, blue for indifferent, and black for bad (George, 1972).

Formal PA probably began in the United States in 1813 when Army General Lewis Cass submitted to the War Department an evaluation of each of his men, described in such colorful terms as "a good-natured man" or "a knave despised by all." Widespread appraisal in the U.S. federal government was first introduced in 1842 (Lopez, 1968).

PA systems in the early twentieth century were used primarily in military and government organizations. The U.S. military, in particular, has been a forerunner in developing PA techniques, including man-to-man ranking, forced-choice measures, and trait-rating scales. Appraisal of industry employees became popular only after World War I, and appraisal of managers was not widely practiced until after World War II.

By the early 1950s, PA was an accepted practice in many organizations. PA was being done in 61% of the businesses surveyed, up 15% from just after World War II (Spriegel, 1962). The type of PA program that existed at this time is illustrated in the following description of a large midwestern utility company.*

The W Department employs 3000 unionized workers, mostly women in clerical positions. Nonsupervisory employees and the lower four levels of supervision are formally rated only when action is to be taken with respect to promotion, discharge, pay changes, etc., or when the Department head requests it. Individuals who reach the top of the rate range for their positions are no longer rated regularly. Nonsupervisors are rated on five characteristics, supervisors on eleven. A rating scale with four categories (excellent, good, fair, and unsatisfactory) is used. The rater, always the

*Thomas L. Whisler & Shirley F. Harper (Eds.), *Performance Appraisal: Research & Practice,* New York: Holt Rinehart & Winston, 1962, p. 456.

immediate superior, is encouraged to write comments in a space provided. The ratings are examined and approved (or additions made) by the rater's supervisor and, in some cases, by a higher manager. The rating form contains a great deal of data not relevant to evaluation, permitting the form to be used for virtually all personnel purposes.

This PA system was typical of this period in several ways:

1 Top management was exempt from appraisal. PA was often applied only to hourly workers; when management was included, it was usually only at the lower levels.
2 Graphic-rating (trait) scales were used (cf. Spriegel, 1962).
3 Only one or two different forms covered all employees appraised.

Another important finding of Whisler's research was the very loose relationship between appraisal results and resulting administrative decisions. Whisler cites case after case in which personnel decisions (e.g., terminations) were independent of or even ran counter to appraisal results: highly rated employees were often fired; low-rated employees, maintained or rehired. "Appraisals are so often made, recorded, filed, and forgotten. Subsequently, decisions involving discrimination among individuals are made, apparently without reference to the periodic evaluations previously made" (Whisler, 1962, p. 476).

A variety of factors may have contributed to this outcome. Personnel and industrial relations departments were relatively weak in most organizations during this period. Employees who were appraised were likely to be hourly workers represented by unions; unions then and now have argued for using seniority-based rather than appraisal-based criteria for administrative decisions. Further, personnel practices regarding exempt employees were considered in-house prerogatives of management that were not subject to legal constraints.

Moreover, ambiguity around PA seems to have led to confusion among supervisors about the purpose of the ratings they gave:

> Many are uncertain as to the ultimate disposition of the rating sheets and as to their importance in terms of the individual employee's progress in the company. That is, most supervisors express ignorance of what "they" do with the ratings once the sheets "go over there" (to the industrial relations department). (Whisler, 1962, p. 450)

Ad hoc appraisals were sometimes used when immediate administrative decisions were needed. Apparently, PA programs were not well understood or taken seriously in many organizations.

PA Reaches the Legal Age

After the passage of the 1964 Civil Rights Act and the 1966 and 1970 Equal Employment Opportunity Commission (EEOC) Guidelines for the regulation of employment selection procedures, legal considerations created strong pressure on organizations to formalize and organize their PA practices. Representatives of major corporations found themselves in court trying to justify (validate) the basis on which salary, promotion, retention, and hiring decisions were made (Feild & Holley, 1975). Because PA ratings were often used for such personnel decisions, they become a source of "selection" information in documenting prima facie evidence of discrimination against protected classes (Odom, 1977). Typical practices of the past, such as the use of personality traits in appraisal, loose correlations between PA ratings and rewards, and the lack of specific job-related behaviors in evaluation were no longer just confusing to managers but also were becoming targets of increasing federal regulation. For its part, the federal government often contributed even more to the confusion by fragmenting efforts to enforce the law. During the late 1960s and 1970s, at least four major federal agencies independently issued guidelines for their jurisdictions that included PA under the rubric of "selection device." These guidelines were not always consistent with one another, and serious attempts by some organizations to comply with these new regulations were fettered with conflicting standards. In response, some organizations gave up efforts to validate their systems (Robertson, 1978).

Still, federal legislation and the civil rights and women's movements of the 1960s and 1970s created the need for rapid improvements in organizational PA practices. PA systems tended to be in constant flux as organizations tried a variety of procedures to cope with the new requirements.

PA in Adulthood—Hybrid Systems and Increased Use of MBO

Although many aspects of PA have remained unchanged over time, some changes in PA practices have been made. Two major trends have been the emergence of sophisticated hybrid systems that incorporate the features of several PA approaches and the increased use of MBO.

RCA Corporation's hybrid appraisal system was discussed at length in a recent survey.* RCA has developed a PA system known as the Talent Inventory that is applicable to 7500 managers in nine major businesses. Each manager is confidentially rated by a group of five to seven employees in his or her "work network" on two dimensions: overall performance and critical incidents. Overall performance is rated by each employee on a scale from

"Exceptional Performer" through "Top Performer," "Effective," and "Satisfactory" to "Not Currently Classified" (unsatisfactory). The critical incidents section is a standardized set of managerial behaviors—e.g., "writes reports that are expert and easily understood"—which each rater then scores from A, for most likely to do, through C, for unlikely, to D, for do not know. Each appraisee then receives an end-of-the-year interview with his or her boss to discuss the appraisal ratings.*

RCA's system points out several innovations in approach uncommon either 25 years ago or today. Most significant are the use of multiple raters, the emphasis on behaviors rather than traits, and the use of training to help managers give feedback to their subordinates. Each of these distinctive features has received attention recently by writers on PA and is discussed in more depth later.

However, some important attributes of the appraisal process remain unchanged in RCA's system. First, each manager is appraised on the basis of a previously established set of dimensions using a standard, numerical scoring system. Second, the focus is on past actions rather than future goals. Third, an appraisal interview is supposed to occur between the manager and his/her immediate supervisor that revolves around these evaluation criteria.

It was a reaction to these attributes that spawned the MBO "revolution" of the 1960s. MBO was first proposed by Peter Drucker in 1954, in *The Practice of Management,* as a result of his study of managerial practices in General Motors. The application of MBO to PA was encouraged by Douglas McGregor's 1957 article, "An Uneasy Look at Performance Appraisal," in which he recommended that employees be appraised on the basis of short-term performance goals, rather than traits, that are set jointly by the employee and the manager. McGregor suggested that this MBO approach to appraisal had the advantages of *(a)* redefining the manager's role to that of helper rather than judge, *(b)* increasing subordinate acceptance, since the emphasis is on performance rather than personality, and *(c)* shifting the orientation toward future actions instead of past behavior.

In 1960, "only a handful of companies" had attempted to establish formal MBO appraisal systems (Patton, 1960, p. 69). Today, a wide variety of MBO appraisal programs have been established in a broad cross section of organizations ranging from General Motors to the Department of Health and Human Services and the Department of Education. The MBO system of Black and Decker is described next (Carroll & Tosi, 1973). The Black and Decker "Overall Performance Work Sheet" contains five parts. Parts A,

*Robert I. Lazer & Walter S. Wikstrom, *Appraising Managerial Performance: Current Practices and Future Directions,* New York: The Conference Board, 1977.

B, and C are filled out independently by the manager and his/her boss and cover personal goals for the year, overall job responsibilities, and specific job targets for the year. Meetings are to be held quarterly, at least to review progress toward work-related goals. Prior to the year-end review, the employee's manager is to complete the last two parts of the form evaluating the factors that have affected job performance and the employee's overall job performance. These factors are then discussed with the subordinate.

In principle, Black and Decker's MBO-oriented approach to appraisal differs from more traditional PA approaches in several important ways:

1 Goals or targets are set for both personal development and for work activities.
2 The employee is then evaluated in terms of accomplishing these goals.
3 Periodic review sessions are prescribed rather than just an annual or semiannual appraisal interview.
4 The employee and the manager engage in an interactive process, with both contributing to goal setting and subsequent evaluation.

THE CURRENT STATUS OF PA: SURVEY RESULTS

Both RCA and Black and Decker have elaborate PA systems for use throughout the organization, and the previous descriptions illustrate how some PA programs were designed and used. This section is intended to give an overall picture of where PA currently stands as a management tool. Results from several recent surveys are summarized to address such questions as How common are formal PA programs? What approaches to evaluation are most often taken? What performance factors are most often rated?

Prevalence of PA Programs

Exhibit 4 summarizes the results from several surveys showing the prevalence of PA programs according to organizational size and type and level within the organization.

Business organizations having a formal PA system ranged from 74% in one study (Lazer & Wikstrom, 1977) to 89% in another (Locher & Teel, 1977). The first figure may be lower, because PA systems for blue-collar and clerical workers were not included in this study. The Lazer and Wikstrom (1977) study showed that between two-thirds and about three-quarters of the companies surveyed had a formal PA program for employees, with some variation by type of industry. Government organizations having PA systems

Exhibit 4 Prevalence of PA Programs (Percentage of Organizations Having a Formal PA Program)

Type of Organization (percentage)		Size of Organization—Businesses Only (percentage)		Level within the Organization—Businesses Only (percentage)	
Study 1 (Lazer & Wikstrom, 1977)		Study 2 (Locher & Teel, 1977)		Study 1 (Lazer & Wikstrom, 1977)	
Manufacturing companies	73	Large organizations	95	Lower management	74
Banks and financial Institutions	78	Small organizations	84	Middle management	71
Insurance companies	67			Upper management	55
Wholesale and retail companies	78				
All companies	74				
Study 2 (Locher & Teel, 1977)					
All companies	89				
Study 3 (Lacho, Stearns, & Villere, 1979)					
City government organizations	76				
Study 4 (Feild & Holley, 1975)					
State government organizations	100				

ranged from 76% in a study of 50 major U.S. city governments (Lacho, Stearns, & Villere, 1979) to 100% in a study of 39 state governments (Feild & Holley, 1975).

Large businesses (more than 500 employees) are apparently more likely than small businesses to have a PA system, but the difference is quite small—95 versus 84% of those surveyed (Locher & Teel, 1977). Finally, PA systems in the businesses surveyed were designed to be used more for lower- (74%) and middle- (71%) management levels than for top management (55%), suggesting that the PA boom has yet to hit the executive suite (Lazer & Wikstrom, 1977). Overall, it is obvious that *PA has become a widely used tool throughout organizations.*

PA Methods Used

The second question concerns the prevalence of various methods for evaluating employee performance. Survey results addressing this question vary widely, depending on the type of organization considered, how the questions are asked, the labels given to various PA methods, and how the results are clustered. However, some general trends are apparent.

In perhaps the most exhaustive survey of managerial PA, Lazer and Wikstrom (1977) found MBO was the most common PA approach in the businesses surveyed, particularly at higher levels of management (63% of PA programs for top management versus 53 and 40% of middle- and lower-management levels, respectively). Essays were the next most common PA method, reported in about 37% of the businesses surveyed throughout all levels of management. Behavioral and trait-rating scales, critical incidents, and checklists were reported used in less than 17% of the businesses.

In another study of businesses, Locher and Teel (1977) found these rankings almost reversed. Of the companies having PA systems, 57% used rating scales, 27% used essays, and only 13% used MBO systems (17% of the larger companies and 9% of the smaller companies). Other PA methods were reported in only 6% of the companies.

Studies of government organizations reveal different patterns still. Lacho, Stearns, and Villere (1979) found in a study of 50 city governments that a combined graphic-rating scale/essay approach was the most common PA method, reported in 68% of the surveyed cities. Rating scales alone accounted for an additional 18% of the cities. Goal-setting and essay methods were reported by only 7 and 5% of the cities, respectively. In a study of 39 state governments, Feild and Holley (1975) found rating scales used by 62% of the organizations. A combined rating scale/essay approach was used by an additional 13% of the states, and 13% used essay methods alone. None of the states reported MBO or other goal-setting methods.

Clearly, there are wide variations in these survey data. Whereas the prevalence of the use of MBO in business is unclear (40–63% in one study versus 13% in another), it is clear that MBO has become an accepted practice in many companies. In contrast, few government agencies have adopted MBO systems. Also, MBO systems are more likely to be used for managers than for hourly and clerical workers (61 versus 19% in businesses surveyed) (Hay Associates, 1976). Moreover, top management is more likely than middle or lower management to be appraised using an MBO system.

Rating scales and essays still abound today in organizations of various sizes and types, although these PA methods are reported less frequently at higher levels of organizations (Hay Associates, 1976). BARS, however, have made only minor inroads (reported by only 8–9% of the businesses in Lazer and Wikstrom's 1977 study). Other PA methods such as critical incidents or rankings were reported rarely, if at all.

Factors Rated in PA

PA forms vary in the specificity of factors to be rated. MBO and essay forms, for instance, leave the selection of performance dimensions up to the manager. Occasionally, the results are amusing, as in the following rogues' gallery of excerpts from military officer efficiency reports.*

> This officer has talents but has kept them well hidden.
>
> Can express a sentence in two paragraphs at a time.
>
> His leadership is outstanding except for his lack of ability to get along with his subordinates.
>
> He has failed to demonstrate any outstanding weaknesses.
>
> Open to suggestions but never follows same.
>
> Never makes the same mistake twice but it seems to me that he has made them all once.
>
> Tends to overestimate himself and underestimate the problem, being surprised and confused by the resulting situations.
>
> An independent thinker with a mediocre mentality.

More often, however, PA forms clearly specify the performance factors on which an employee is to be rated. Several researchers have examined the actual PA forms used by organizations, and the results of these examinations are particularly helpful in understanding what organizations are trying to measure with PA. Some of these results are shown in Exhibit 5.

Lazer and Wikstrom (1977) found 10 factors most commonly used on PA forms in business organizations, ranging from 49 of the 61 organizations surveyed for "knowledge of work" to 28 for "evaluation and development of personnel." In their study of state governments, Feild and Holley (1975) analyzed supervisory and nonsupervisory forms separately but found only small differences between them. Many of the same items showed up in both surveys, albeit with different frequencies. The findings of both surveys show that *PA forms still emphasize broadly defined traits rather than specific behaviors or performance outcomes.* For instance, six of the 10 most commonly rated factors in business may be seen as personality traits (leadership, initiative, cooperation, judgment, creativity, and dependability), and the other four factors are behaviors or outcomes defined in very global terms (e.g., quality and quantity of work). This is striking, given the amount of criticism trait approaches have received in recent years and the emphasis in the literature since the 1960s on MBO- and BARS-oriented approaches to PA.

*Thomas H. Patten, Jr., *Pay: Employee Compensation and Incentive Plans,* New York: Macmillan, 1977, p. 357.

Purposes of PA

Earlier studies of PA (e.g., Whisler, 1962) showed that when PA ratings were used in an organization, it was on an ad hoc basis for administrative purposes—for instance, to justify the company's position in grievance cases.

Exhibit 5 Factors Rated in PA

Businesses[a]

Factor	Percentage of Companies Surveyed
Knowledge of work	80
Leadership, influence	62
Initiative	62
Quality of work, accuracy	61
Quantity of work	56
Cooperation	56
Judgment	54
Creativity, resourcefulness, innovativeness	51
Dependability	51
Evaluation and development of personnel	46

State Government Organizations[b]

Variable Factor	Included on Supervisory Forms (percentage)	Included on Non-supervisory Forms (percentage)
Quality of work	59	67
Quantity of work	49	56
Initiative	44	49
Human relations	41	33
Judgment	36	28
Job knowledge	33	39
Work habits	33	33
Dependability	31	42
Organizing and planning	31	not included
Supervisory ability	21	not included
Cooperation	not included	26
Attendance	not included	26

[a]*Appraising Managerial Performance: Current Practices and Future Directions,* Robert I. Lazer and Walter S. Wikstrom, © 1977 The Conference Board.
[b]Hubert S. Feild and William H. Holley, "Performance Appraisal—An Analysis of State-Wide Practice," *Public Personnel Management,* May–June 1975, p. 148.

Exhibit 6 Uses of PA in the 1970s[a]

Use	Lazer and Wikstrom (1977) (percentage)	Bureau of National Affairs (1974) (percentage)	Lacho, Stearns, & Villere (1979) (percentage)
Counseling	("Performance feedback": 73–82)	("Setting goals": 57)	
Salary administration	63–70	85	80
Promotion	50–66	64	74
Training and development	54–60	55	Development: 62 Assess training needs: 44
Retention and discharge			Dismissal: 69 Demotion: 64
Manpower planning	23–34	37	
Validation of selection techniques	12–13	23	23

[a]*Appraising Managerial Performance: Current Practices and Future Directions,* Robert I. Lazer and Walter S. Wikstrom, © 1977 The Conference Board.

Events in the past several decades have provided the impetus for a different set of PA uses. In 1957, McGregor first proposed that PA be used for counseling and developing employees. Drucker (1954) and Odiorne (1965) raised the possibility that MBO could be a tool for organizational planning. More recently, the courts have made PA a necessary tool in the organization's arsenal against discrimination lawsuits. This section addresses the extent to which these forces have changed how PA is used in organizations.

Exhibit 6 summarizes the results of three recent surveys on how PA is used. Administrative uses of PA still predominate. The use of PA in salary decisions ranged from 63–85% of the organizations surveyed, use in promotion decisions from 50–74%, and use in retention and discharge decisions from 58–69%. The use of PA in counseling activities was also high (57–82% of the organizations surveyed), as well as use in training and development decisions (44–62% of the organizations surveyed).

The recent trend toward use of PA in human resource planning is reflected in the first two studies (23–37% of the organizations surveyed). Increasing pressure to use PA for legal documentation is only partly substantiated by these surveys: responses from only 12–23% of the organizations cited use of PA for validating selection techniques. Those figures will no doubt increase as organizations come to recognize the usefulness of PA as a medium for legal documentation.

Overall, *the purposes for which PA is reportedly used have expanded considerably over the past 25 years*. The following uses of PA were all cited in several organizations: administrative decisions (salary, promotion, retention and discharge); counseling; training and development; human resource planning; and validation studies.

Effectiveness of PA Programs

One of the most important, yet unanswered, questions is whether PA systems are effective in accomplishing their purposes. With few exceptions (e.g., Ivancevich, 1974), researchers have prescribed PA systems without evaluating how well they work. Evaluating the impact of an organizational intervention on organizational performance is an extremely difficult task, given the number of factors that can confound results. For instance, to what extent can improved performance be traced to the new PA system, or to changed market conditions, or to internal changes that are a routine part of organizational life? What sort of time lag should one expect before the impact of PA is felt? What areas of performance are most likely to be affected?

Of the several studies that do address this issue, most used self-reported "satisfaction" or "effectiveness" measures in lieu of observable performance measures—perhaps paralleling the preponderance of PA systems measuring traits rather than behavioral or outcome dimensions. The results of surveys approaching PA effectiveness in this way must be viewed with caution, especially since respondents were, for the most part, the same human resource professionals who designed and administered the PA programs. Lazer and Wikstrom (1977) found that 66% of lower-management PA systems, 63% of middle-management systems, and 71% of top-management systems were reported effective. The newer the PA system was, the more likely it was to be reported as effective (for instance, 93% of the PA systems for top management that had been in use for less than a year was reported effective versus only 67% of those in use three or more years). This finding may indicate declining enthusiasm for a PA system following its initial introduction.

Lazer and Wikstrom also reported their findings on the comparative effectiveness of different PA systems. MBO was rated effective in 75% of the organizations using it, whereas each of the other PA systems used (essays, rating scales, etc.) was reported effective in less than half of the organizations surveyed. The widespread dissatisfaction with PA systems, even among human resource professionals, is striking. Clearly, it is time to take stock of PA as an organizational tool and to explore ways to improve its effectiveness.

Caveats on Survey Findings

Survey evidence is not infallible, and there are several reasons to view the survey data presented here with caution. Most survey studies involve sending a single questionnaire to the head of an organization's human resource department. We have found that organizations, particularly large ones, rarely have a single, unified PA policy. PA forms, documentation procedures, and purposes all tend to differ among and even within divisions and departments of companies. It is difficult for a survey respondent to capture this variety on a single questionnaire.

Also, PA practices are often far removed from the policies that human resource professionals believe are being carried out. Porter, Lawler, and Hackman (1975) described a phenomenon that they call the "vanishing" PA:

> When interviewed separately, subordinates report that they have not had a performance appraisal session for several years, while superiors report they hold regular performance appraisal sessions. Further investigation typically reveals that the superiors at some point in time have talked in rather general terms with the subordinates about their performance. The superiors consider this to be a performance appraisal session, but the subordinates do not and wonder why they are not getting the kind of feedback they want. (p. 320)

Managers are often confused about corporate and divisional PA policy and about how to complete the form and conduct a PA interview. And managers often believe that top management does not consider PA an important issue. The result is predictable: PA practices in an organization differ dramatically from the policy and procedure manuals. Again, the survey respondent may not know or may not indicate how PA is actually carried out.

Another point to remember is that the purposes that human resource managers see for PA are not necessarily the same as the purposes managers and employees have in mind. For managers, PA may be not so much a tool for organizational planning or legal documentation as it is a forum for discussion with subordinates or for improving unit performance. For employees, PA can serve as a feedback channel to let them know how they are doing and to learn where they stand in the organization. The fact that the uses of PA often vary from human resource professionals to managers to employees puts tension on the PA system, since, as we see subsequently, not all purposes are served equally well by any one PA system. And these distinctions are not always reflected in survey data.

Survey findings can provide some insight into PA policies and procedures, but the limits of these findings in providing an accurate picture of PA should be understood. Different research methods are needed to answer many questions about PA policies and practices.

IN CONCLUSION

> The context in which the manager makes personnel decisions today is very different from what it was, say, in 1940. (Sloan & Johnson, 1968, p. 15)

A little over a decade ago, Sloan and Johnson (1968) outlined the trends they saw in PA policy:

1 An enlarged scope as PA becomes seen as a part of a larger organizational system.
2 Use of PA more as a tool for corporate planning and less for controlling performance via administrative decisions.
3 Greater psychometric sophistication in appraisal theory and methods.

Although we strongly agree with Sloan and Johnson in their leading quote—the context of personnel decisions has indeed changed markedly in the past 40 years—the analysis in this chapter suggests that they are only partly right in their interpretations of specific PA trends.

The "enlarged scope" of today's PA is reflected primarily in the increasing number of demands being placed on PA systems. PA was once called on solely for use in administrative decisions, but it is now being used for many purposes, ranging from counseling and employee development to documentation of the organization's position in Equal Employment Opportunity lawsuits. Only recently, in some MBO and hybrid PA systems, have attempts been made to establish PA as a foundation for broader personnel and organizational systems.

Sloan and Johnson's second point, that the use of PA for administrative decisions has declined, is simply not borne out by the survey evidence. Instead, we find that administrative uses are still common but that other uses have been added to it.

The third trend, toward greater psychometric sophistication, is supported by the recent introduction of new PA methods such as BARS. Again, however, whereas increasingly sophisticated systems have been added to the PA arsenal, old "tried-and-true" systems like essay forms and crude trait scales are still used in many organizations.

THE BOTTOM LINE

After completing this trip through the history of PA it makes sense to ask, "So what?" What, if any, implications does this look at PA practices—past and present—have for you and your organization? There are several:

PA is on center stage If you find yourself focusing on PA with an interest in updating or improving it, it is no accident. Nor is this emphasis misplaced. You are part of a major trend in U.S. organizations to conduct formal PA on more of your employees. This emphasis on PA is a healthy, constructive response to various pressures (including legal guidelines).

PA is a tool for all seasons If you are less than satisfied with the PA system in your organization, you are not alone among human resource managers. One reason for your disaffection might be the several and perhaps conflicting uses you have assigned to PA. What started out as a simple, annual exercise to help make administrative decisions has become a tool for directing and motivating employees, planning for future managerial talent, and even protecting the organization against legal threats regarding personnel actions. If you expect PA to do all or most of these things, it is no wonder it is found wanting.

PA practices—whom do you ask? If this chapter still leaves you wondering how PA is done in the organization, you are not alone here either. Most reviews of PA practices rely on the word of PA designers and implementers. What the field needs, and what you need in your organization, is a more direct assessment of PA that involves asking the clients themselves (both the managers and subordinates) if they are doing PA, how they are doing PA, and how useful PA is to them. Both the PA research, and often organizations as well, have been avoiding direct, client-oriented evaluations of PA systems. Although such evaluations are risky, they are a critical first step in making changes likely to improve your PA system.

3

Performance Appraisal as a Measurement Process

It is the physician's business to know that circular wounds heal more slowly, the geometer's to know the reason why. (Aristotle, *Posterior Analytics,* 79a14)

My appraisal didn't seem to reflect that any form or set of criteria was used to gauge my performance. My manager just briefly mentioned strengths and weaknesses verbally off the top of the head. (Professional, manufacturing firm)

I wish my manager would go over step-by-step the details on my appraisal so I could find out the areas he used to judge me. I really had no idea how he came to the conclusion that he had, except at the end I was told I did a fine job. But what areas did he use? (Manager, manufacturing firm)

In the past, the design of many PA systems began and ended by answering one question: "What form should we use?" Those idyllic days of simplicity are gone. Today's designers and users of PA systems are confronted both internally and externally with a seemingly endless barrage of perplexing questions such as these:

1. Is the system valid?
2. Are the ratings reliable?
3. Are the performance dimensions job related?
4. How are these numbers going to be used?
5. Does the distribution of scores indicate evidence of discrimination?
6. How will these numbers be explained to employees?
7. Does the system distinguish the high performers from the average performers?
8. Are the scales well anchored?
9. What type of job analysis was conducted?

These types of questions have created extreme frustration in organizations, because PA practitioners and designers, much like Aristotle's physician, are typically unfamiliar with the psychometric issues such questions address and may not see their relevance to finding the "right form."

Recent legal pressures and expanded uses of PA data have thrust psychometric issues on the user and, in doing so, have substantially heightened the organizational costs of approaching PA wth naiveté. Today's reality makes psychometric issues surrounding performance measurement more relevant than ever before, and the need for informed PA users and designers is increasingly critical to organizational effectiveness.

In addressing PA as a measurement process, this chapter examines those aspects of PA that have received the most attention from psychologists and psychometricians over the past 25 years. Several recent reviews of the measurement literature have reflected changes over time in both definitions of job performance criteria and procedures for measuring these criteria in PA systems (DeCotiis & Petit, 1978; Ivancevich, Szilagyi, & Wallace, 1977; Kane & Lawler, 1979; Landy & Farr, 1980; Wexley, 1979). The five sections of this chapter explore these changes by (*a*) examining definitions of the key concepts of performance and performance measurement, (*b*) presenting criteria for evaluating performance measurement approaches, (*c*) highlighting major legal issues surrounding PA systems, (*d*) outlining and evaluating major measurement approaches currently in PA systems, and (*e*) discussing organizational implications of PA measurement issues.

JOB PERFORMANCE AND PERFORMANCE MEASUREMENT

Most PA systems are designed to measure individual job performance. Whereas ultimate performance is reflected most frequently through group or larger unit output (e.g., profit margin or return on investment), PA usually is associated with individual output.

Defining job performance in an organization at the level of the individual contributor is a difficult process, accomplished only by making certain assumptions about the performance criteria to be evaluated:

Assumption 1: The nature of job performance is such that every individual can be held independently accountable for output by the organization.
Assumption 2: The organization can specify desirable or undesirable individual job performance in relation to organizational goals. Individual job performance is measurable.
Assumption 3: Individual performance varies significantly among and within jobs.

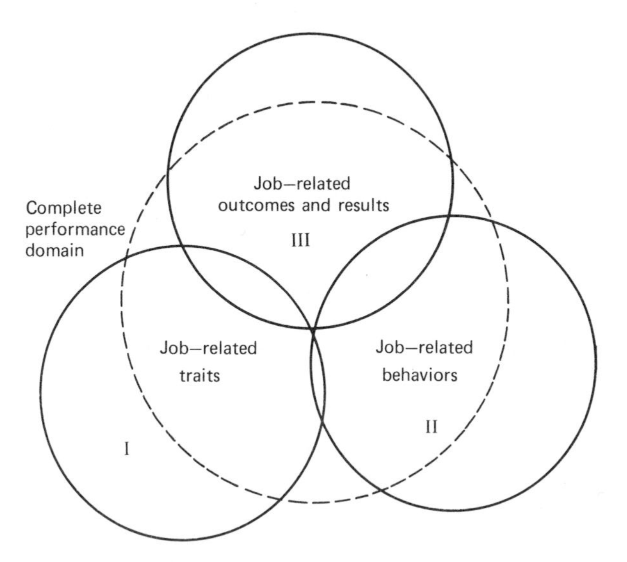

Figure 2 Categories of PA content.

Assumption 4: Individual job performance is not only measurable and variable but also changeable through development, motivation, or replacement of the job incumbent.

There are three basic categories of individual PA performance content: individual personality traits, behaviors, and outcomes. These three categories, representing the measurable domain of individual job performance, are illustrated in Figure 2. Because the "true domain" of job performance is approximated but never reached, it is shown as a dotted circle; the three solid-line subcircles, representing measurable traits, behaviors, and outcomes, overlap with but are not equivalent to either each other or the true domain. Possible examples of each of these three performance content categories for managers are:

1 ***Personality traits***
 - **a** Leadership.
 - **b** Initiative.
 - **c** Attitude.

2 ***Behaviors***
 - **a** Organized employee feedback sessions.
 - **b** Presented report clearly and concisely at trade association meeting.
 - **c** Responded to customer complaints promptly and thoroughly.

3 ***Outcomes***

a Reduced unit absenteeism by 5%.
b Completed development of a new product line before deadline.
c Increased net sales by 7%.

The success of PA measurement rests first on the extent to which job performance criteria, the performance domain, can be specified. Each of the content areas (traits, behaviors, and outcomes) focuses on different definitions of performance criteria and suggests a different measurement approach. Defining the content of a job using these three categories is done through either formal job analysis procedures or, more typically, through a less systematized, more formal process. Job performance is not a singular, unidimensional concept. In fact, job performance criteria are so abundant and complex that different PA programs with different purposes may focus on different aspects of job performance. Thus job performance involves defining *what criteria* are to be measured.

Although job performance involves identifying appropriate criteria, performance measurement involves how performance criteria, once defined, will actually be measured. If most actual job performance criteria were objectively measurable (as in the classic example, "number of widgets produced"), these would constitute a nearly ideal set of performance criteria. However, it is difficult to get objective performance measures for many jobs (Landy & Farr, 1980). And in most organizations, managerial and professional job performance is not typically measured but is evaluated or appraised (Patten, 1977). Therefore, PA is a formal process of observing and evaluating individual employees' performance. The PA process assumes that job performance can be defined rigorously enough to be observed and assessed accurately, even if it cannot be objectively measured (Patten, 1977).

Most organizations, in fact, do depend on judgmental indices of job performance for performance measurement (Landy & Farr, 1980). When judgmental indices are introduced (and, indeed, these represent the majority of PA measures), the PA measurement process becomes susceptible to numerous problems of rater accuracy and dependability. The effectiveness of most PA programs rests in large part on the ability of the rater, typically the supervisor, to make accurate judgments about job performance that are based on sound job-related criteria and systematic collection of information related to those criteria. To adequately address the issue of PA accuracy, today's PA designer must look to psychometric and legal guidelines for direction.

PSYCHOMETRIC ISSUES IN PERFORMANCE MEASUREMENT

The literature suggests at least four psychometric issues important to any effective performance measurement approach: validity, reliability, discriminability, and usefulness for PA purposes.

Validity

How accurate and relevant are the performance dimensions measured? The psychometric and legal core of effective PA measurement focuses on the issue of validity—the clear demonstration that performance measures are related to job performance and measure what is intended to be assessed (Lazer, 1976). Three types of validity have been emphasized.

Criterion-related validity involves the degree to which performance measures predict important elements of expected job performance. Traditionally, supervisors' PA ratings have been used in studies as criterion measures to validate other employment procedures and tests. Thus to treat PA ratings as a test to be validated requires finding an even better approximation of job performance than PA itself. Of course, this "more ultimate approximation" might also have to be validated against an "even more ultimate measure." Therefore, as most PA measures for managerial and professional personnel are assumed to be the ultimate measures, the strategy of criterion-related validity becomes an extremely difficult one to accomplish and, in fact, may have only limited applicability to PA ratings (Kane & Lawler, 1979).

Construct validity involves the degree to which a PA measurement technique assesses a specific characteristic, personality trait, or theoretical concept deemed to be essential to job performance. The existence of such a construct (like interpersonal effectiveness, sensitivity to others, or initiative) is usually determined in one or both of two ways: (*a*) the degree to which differences between performance dimension measures are sufficient to consider them as distinct constructs (discriminant validity) or (*b*) the degree to which multiple approaches designed to measure the same construct actually produce similar measurement results (convergent validity). Construct validity remains the most elusive of all the validity approaches. There seems to be limited agreement in the literature on definitions of either "construct" or "construct validity" (Norton, Balloun, & Konstantinovich, 1980). Although personality traits are still frequently used as constructs for performance measurement, their use is suspect, because no validation procedure is universally accepted.

Content validity involves the degree to which the performance criteria represent the content of the job performed. Thus content validity, often referred to as job relevance, addresses whether the job performance domain has been adequately sampled.

In general, the determination of job relevance is concerned with three issues (Kane & Lawler, 1979; Wexley, 1979): measurement deficiency, measurement contamination, and measurement distortion. *Measurement deficiency* involves the degree to which job performance measures exclude some performance dimensions considered to be important and representative of expected performance standards for the job. *Measurement contamination* involves the degree to which performance measures include some irrelevant performance dimensions that are not related to expected performance standards important for a particular job. *Measurement distortion* involves the degree to which relevant job performance standards are represented but are weighted disproportionately from their true importance in effective job performance.

For PA ratings in particular, the importance of job relevance has been underscored in recent court cases involving the legal requirements of Title VII of the 1964 Civil Rights Act and the *Uniform Guidelines on Employee Selection Procedures* (Kleiman & Faley, 1978; Odom, 1979). When PA ratings are used as a basis for administrative decisions, they are considered tests or employee selection procedures under the *Guidelines* and are "most amenable to the content validation strategy" (Odom, 1979, p. 2). For example, the *Guidelines* state that:

> To demonstrate content validity of a [PA] procedure, a user should show that the behaviors demonstrated in the selection procedure provide a representative sample of the work products of the job. (EEOC, 1978, Section 14.C.4)

Perhaps even more significant, the *Guidelines* emphasize:

> There should be a job analysis which includes an analysis of the important work behaviors required for successful performance and their relative importance. . . . Any job analysis should focus on work behavior(s) and the tasks associated with them. (EEOC, 1978, Section 14.C.2)

Prien (1975) summarized two broadly defined approaches to job analysis—the *worker-oriented* and *task-oriented* approaches. In worker-oriented approaches, job-knowledgeable employees are asked to make judgments about the knowledge and abilities (and sometimes personality characteristics) involved in effective job performance. Examples of such approaches include the job element method (Primoff, 1972) and the Position Analysis Questionnaire (McCormick, Jeanneret, & Mecham, 1969). In task-oriented approaches, job-knowledgeable employees are asked to describe the activities an employee performs on the job. An example of this approach is the Executive Position Description Questionnaire (Hemphill, 1960).

Therefore, whereas the ultimate, or true measures of managerial and professional job performance appear to be ideals that are not readily identifiable or totally quantifiable, job-knowledgeable employees can provide rigorous judgments about the nature of the job performance domain (Wexley, 1979). In doing this, both the psychometric and legal criteria for effective PA measures can be met.

Reliability

How stable and consistent are the measurement results? Measurement results are usually considered reliable when they remain stable from one rating period to another or consistent from rater to rater (Smith, 1976; Wexley, 1979). Normally, instability over time and inconsistencies among raters are termed measurement "error" or "noise." In the case of performance measurement in an on-the-job context, Kane and Lawler (1979) have noted that these concepts require further examination in terms of their actual applicability.

Stability, or *test-retest reliability,* involves the degree of measurement consistency between occasions and assumes that the rater, employee, and purposes of appraisal remain stable from one evaluation situation to another. In practice, this is rarely the case and may be an inappropriate criterion for evaluating PA measurement strategies.

Interrater reliability involves the degree of consistency between PA raters. This concept assumes that any two or three raters have equivalent knowledge of an employee's performance. However, this is probably not the case in organizational practice, since supervisors, peers, and others see different aspects of job performance.

Internal consistency involves the consistency between measures of the same performance domain and determines the degree to which a particular performance construct (and not several others) is being assessed by a designated measure of that construct.

Discriminability

Does the measurement approach actually reflect differences in performance? Discriminability is a critical assumption of PA that involves the degree to which a performance measure actually distinguishes among individual employees in terms of performance (Wexley, 1979) and that results in a distribution of employees according to level of performance. *Operational discriminability* occurs when the actual use of a measurement instrument successfully distinguishes employees according to performance (Kane & Lawler, 1979). With very subjective rating scales, requiring a high degree of inference on the part of the rater, three errors can occur that affect, or bias, operational discriminability:

Leniency error occurs when the PA rater artificially assigns all (certain groups of) employees high performance ratings, and all (certain) scores cluster at top levels of the measurement instrument. *Strictness error* occurs when the PA rater artificially assigns all (certain groups of) employees low performance ratings, and all (certain) scores cluster at the bottom levels of the measurement instrument. *Central tendency error* occurs when raters artificially assign all (certain groups of) employees moderate or average performance ratings, and all (certain) scores cluster at the middle levels of the measurement instrument.

Structural discriminability involves the degree to which the measurement instrument itself is able to reflect the performance differences that actually exist in the employee population. Three aspects of structural discriminability have been discussed by Kane and Lawler (1979): *Score ratio* involves the number of performance level rating choices available in relation to how many distinctive performance levels actually exist in the employee population being appraised. *Uncertainty* involves the degree to which the measurement scale provides information: Are there enough response choices in the area where many employees tend to cluster so that important differences can be captured? *Profile distribution* involves the degree to which a given scale reflects an individual's distribution of performance over time or situations versus an average reflected in one response level. (All common PA measures require only the single "average" measure.)

Usefulness

How helpful are the measurement results in accomplishing the purposes of a PA system? As seen in Chapter 2, the ratings or measurement results obtained in PA are put to a variety of uses. McCall and DeVries (1977) have suggested that these uses place some unique demands on the measurement approach. It is possible that a measurement strategy would meet all the previously cited criteria and yet falter in serving various uses.

Data from PA measures may be used as input to a variety of decisions involving compensation, termination, and promotion. Using data from individual goal-setting procedures, for example, may not be as helpful in determining salary increases as a measurement approach that provides a relative rating of performance for employees throughout an organization. Another major use of PA measurement data involves sharing the data as feedback to employees. In this case, performance improvement, motivation, or development requires that the performance criteria and evaluation data are concrete and easily understandable to both managers and employees.

In considering these four criteria for PA measurement approaches—validity, reliability, discriminability, and usefulness—the PA literature has heavily emphasized formal psychometric properties (DeCotiis & Petit, 1978; Schwab, Heneman, & DeCotiis, 1975; Smith, 1976). In doing so, the literature has at times reflected the knowledge gap between controlled laboratory findings and the difficulties of application in practice.

LEGAL ISSUES IN PERFORMANCE MEASUREMENT

Before proceeding with a discussion of existing measurement options, it is necessary to examine some of the legal issues of PA. The reason such a discussion follows a description of psychometric issues in a chapter about measurement may not be obvious. In reality, however, the legal guidelines for PA are actually an affirmation of professional principles for sound assessment developed by professionals themselves (American Psychological Association, 1974; Division of Industrial-Organizational Psychology, 1975).

The current guidelines, in essence, require any test or selection device showing adverse impact to be validated or proved to be related to job performance. This has been, and will continue to be, as much sound psychological and psychometric practice as legal compliance. Yet it seems that it has taken a legal examination of the impact of certain personnel decisions, like PA, to establish consistent standards of practice and stable conceptual frameworks (i.e., PA is a selection device, not just a criterion measure).

The Tower Amendment to the 1964 Civil Rights Act was the first in a continuing series of events to alter the legal context of PA. Specifically, the Tower Amendment approved the use of "professionally developed ability tests" for employment decisions, provided that such tests were not "designed, intended, or used to discriminate because of race, color, religion, sex, or national origin" (Robertson, 1978). EEOC was given legislative responsibility for enforcing this act. In 1966, the EEOC issued guidelines regarding an employer's obligation for testing and selection procedures pertaining to equal employment opportunity. These guidelines were substantially revised in 1970.

In 1971, the Supreme Court handed down a landmark decision in *Griggs v. Duke Power,* incorporating the existing guidelines into a legal framework for employment testing. In essence, the Supreme Court gave legitimacy to guidelines which required that employers produce evidence that selection criteria are related to actual job performance and put the burden of proof on employers to demonstrate nondiscrimination in the presence of adverse impact.

Promotion, retention, and selection decisions were the focus of early court cases involving these guidelines, and PA ratings seemed to serve more as the criteria against which employment decisions were validated rather than being viewed as selection devices or tests themselves (Lazer, 1976). *Brito v. Zia Company* (1973), however, established the applicability of the guidelines to PA ratings as well. In this case, involving layoffs of Spanish-surnamed employees, the court concluded that:

1 Supervisory ratings were vague and subjective measures.
2 The appraisers (supervisors) did not have regular, reasonable, daily contact with employees.
3 Supervisor performance ratings, as selection devices resulting in layoffs, were not scored and administered under appropriately standardized and controlled conditions.

In 1975, the Supreme Court handed down an opinion in *Albemarle Paper Company v. Moody* that upheld the provisions of the extensively revised 1970 guidelines. The court criticized three particular aspects of the testing program:

1 Using subjective supervisory ratings as criteria.
2 Using a test validated only on upper-level positions for entry-level jobs.
3 Validating a test on a group that is not representative of job applicants.

In essence, *Albemarle v. Moody* was the landmark decision that legally required supervisors to use more than vague and subjective criteria in reaching employment decisions and prescribed statistical validation procedures to establish proof of job relatedness.

Washington v. Davis (1976) appeared initially to dilute the growing impact of the EEOC *Guidelines* by refocusing on the need to prove intent to discriminate. The court decided in favor of a police selection procedure that resulted in disproportionate numbers of blacks failing but which showed no intent to discriminate against black applicants. The dilution, however, did not occur. *Washington v. Davis* had been tried under the Constitution (that requires proof of intent) rather than Title VII (which does not). The Title VII framework remained intact and gained momentum through the 1970s.

Also during the 1970s, however, another set of guidelines based on the EEOC model was established by the Office of Federal Contract Compliance. Although similar, these two sets of guidelines differed in the degree of stringency and, in a few cases, actually contradicted each other

(Robertson, 1978). The result was that several sets of standards were required for employers instead of just one. Whereas the EEOC still maintained responsibility for enforcement of Title VII legislation, the Civil Service Commission, the Department of Justice, and the Department of Labor also enforced antidiscrimination regulations.

On August 25, 1978, the *Uniform Guidelines on Employee Selection Procedures* were adopted by the four major federal enforcement agencies (EEOC, 1978). These *Guidelines* replaced existing requirements and have provided one consistent set of federal regulations.

The *Guidelines,* building on past regulations, include the following:

1 Employers may not, through the use of any selection device for employment decisions, discriminate against any group protected by Title VII of the Civil Rights Act of 1964 (i.e., on the basis of race, color, religion, sex, or national origin).
2 Employment decisions are any personnel practices that result in selection, training, transfer, retention, or promotion of employees.
3 It is not necessary to establish an *intent* to discriminate to prove discrimination. The presence (or absence) of a disproportionate number from a protected group is defined as prima facie evidence of adverse impact.

The new *Guidelines* include a specific rule of thumb for evaluating adverse impact—the four-fifths, or 80%, rule. The 80% rule states that the selection ratio for protected groups must not fall below 80% of the selection ratio for the majority group. In other words, there is a 20% buffer zone for selection rate differences; but a difference beyond 20% constitutes a prima facie case of adverse impact.

Further, the *Guidelines* do not require validation documentation in all cases—just those cases where the test or selection device (e.g., PA ratings) results in adverse impact on a protected group. For cases in which validation is required, the *Guidelines* recognize content and construct validity as equally acceptable validation options as criterion (empirical) validity evidence.

Also, the *Guidelines* have added the concept of a "bottom-line strategy" to limit the need to validate at each step of any personnel selection procedure. The *Guidelines* state that as long as the combined effect of a selection process (e.g., a PA system) does not produce adverse impact, each selection step does not have to be validated separately. In return for this reduction in required validation steps, organizations must now keep records of application and hiring statistics separately by protected group.

Finally, the *Guidelines* appear to be going one step beyond "equal opportunity" by allowing employers to choose alternative selection devices that eliminate adverse impact rather than retaining devices for which differences have been validated. Robertson (1978) views this as a move toward a "concept of equal results."

Several authors have reviewed the *Guidelines* and recent court cases involving PA measures (Cascio & Bernardin, in press; Holley, Feild, & Barnett, 1976; Odom, 1977). In general, these cases point to the following legal requirements for PA systems:

1 PA ratings should be job related and valid.
2 Job-related performance criteria to be rated should be derived from a thorough job analysis that appropriately represents all significant performance dimensions.
3 PA ratings should be collected under formal standardized conditions.
4 PA ratings should be examined for bias (evidence of adverse impact). Care should be taken—through measurement development, training, and ongoing review—to eliminate bias regarding race, color, sex, religion, and national origin.
5 Organizations should avoid use of supervisory ratings based on vague and subjective factors.
6 PA raters must have personal knowledge and reasonable contact with the job performance to be rated; they must be able to make the appropriate observations.

Thus, from both a psychometric and legal perspective, organizations today do not have the luxury of deciding whether to examine psychometric properties of existing PA programs. The real choice is in selecting among alternative approaches available.

PERFORMANCE MEASUREMENT SYSTEMS—CURRENT OPTIONS

It is useful for any organization to develop a broader perspective on the approaches available to measure job performance. Such a perspective might lead an organization to (*a*) select a different technique, (*b*) supplement its existing approach with another technique, or (*c*) retain its existing approach with a better understanding of its strengths and weaknesses.

Existing reviews of the PA literature vary widely in both the number of measurement approaches explored and the basis for comparing or contrasting these techniques. Since no single schema seems compelling, the authors have generated an overview of existing measurement approaches based on three categories:

1 Type of measurement criteria (content).
   a Global effectiveness (unspecified).
   b Traits.
   c Behaviors.
   d Outcomes.
2 Number of measurement criteria.
   a Unidimensional.
   b Multidimensional.
3 Degree of inference or judgment required by the rater to generate measurement data.
   a High.
   b Medium.
   c Low.

Within this structure, seven measurement approaches are reviewed, as outlined in Exhibit 7.

Exhibit 7 Measurement Approaches

Level of Inference Required	Unidimensional	Multidimensional		
	Global	Traits	Behaviors	Outcomes
High	Global rating or Essay Ranking procedures	Graphic-rating scales		
	—		Critical incident methods BARS	
Medium				
	—			Objective and Goal setting
Low				Organizational records

Strategy 1: Global essays and ratings This strategy for measuring job performance is cited in literature reviews (Cummings & Schwab, 1973; Schneier & Beatty, 1979) and often found in organizational practice (Lacho, Stearns, & Villere, 1979; Lazer & Wikstrom, 1977; Locher & Teel, 1977). In

Exhibit 8 Traditional Rating Scale

AD-XXX (1-75)

UNITED STATES DEPARTMENT OF AGRICULTURE

EMPLOYEE APPRAISAL

INSTRUCTIONS: Section B to be completed by the appraiser; and Section C to be completed by employee.

SECTION A – GENERAL INFORMATION

1. NAME (Last, First, Middle)	2. SOCIAL SECURITY NUMBER	3. AGENCY	4. PAY PLAN	5. OCCUPATIONAL SERIES	6. GRADE/STEP
7. TITLE OF POSITION	8. POSITION NUMBER	9. STANDARD JOB NUMBER		10. PERIOD COVERED BY APPRAISAL FROM: TO:	
11. DUTY STATION		12. ORGANIZATION			

SECTION B – APPRAISAL FACTORS:

Rate the employee on those factors that apply. Write N/A in the box for the factors not applicable. Explain or define each rating by supplying an example or description. *(A brief phrase or sentence will suffice.)*	APPRAISAL LEVEL				
	LOW 1	AVE 2	3	4	HIGH 5
1. ACCEPTING RESPONSIBILITY AND INITIATING ACTION:	LOW	AVE	3	4	HIGH
2. EVALUATING FACTS AND MAKING DECISIONS:	LOW	AVE	3	4	HIGH
3. ADAPTABILITY:	LOW	AVE	3	4	HIGH
4. INNOVATING.	LOW	AVE	3	4	HIGH
5. PROBLEM SOLVING:	LOW	AVE	3	4	HIGH
6. PLANNING AND ORGANIZING:	LOW	AVE	3	4	HIGH

7. EXECUTING ASSIGNED PLANS AND FOLLOWING INSTRUCTIONS:	LOW	AVE	3	4	HIGH
8. COMMUNICATING ORALLY	LOW	AVE	3	4	HIGH
9. COMMUNICATING IN WRITING	LOW	AVE	3	4	HIGH
10. GETTING ALONG WITH PEOPLE:	LOW	AVE	3	4	HIGH

11. EMPLOYEE POTENTIAL:

12. SPECIAL SKILLS (*Describe specific abilities of this employee which you believe may be helpful in placement decisions.*)

SIGNATURE OF APPRAISER	DATE	**NOTICE:** If the employee you are appraising is your immediate subordinate, you are responsible for having the employee complete the employee availability and career objectives statement on the reverse.

Exhibit 8 Traditional Rating Scale

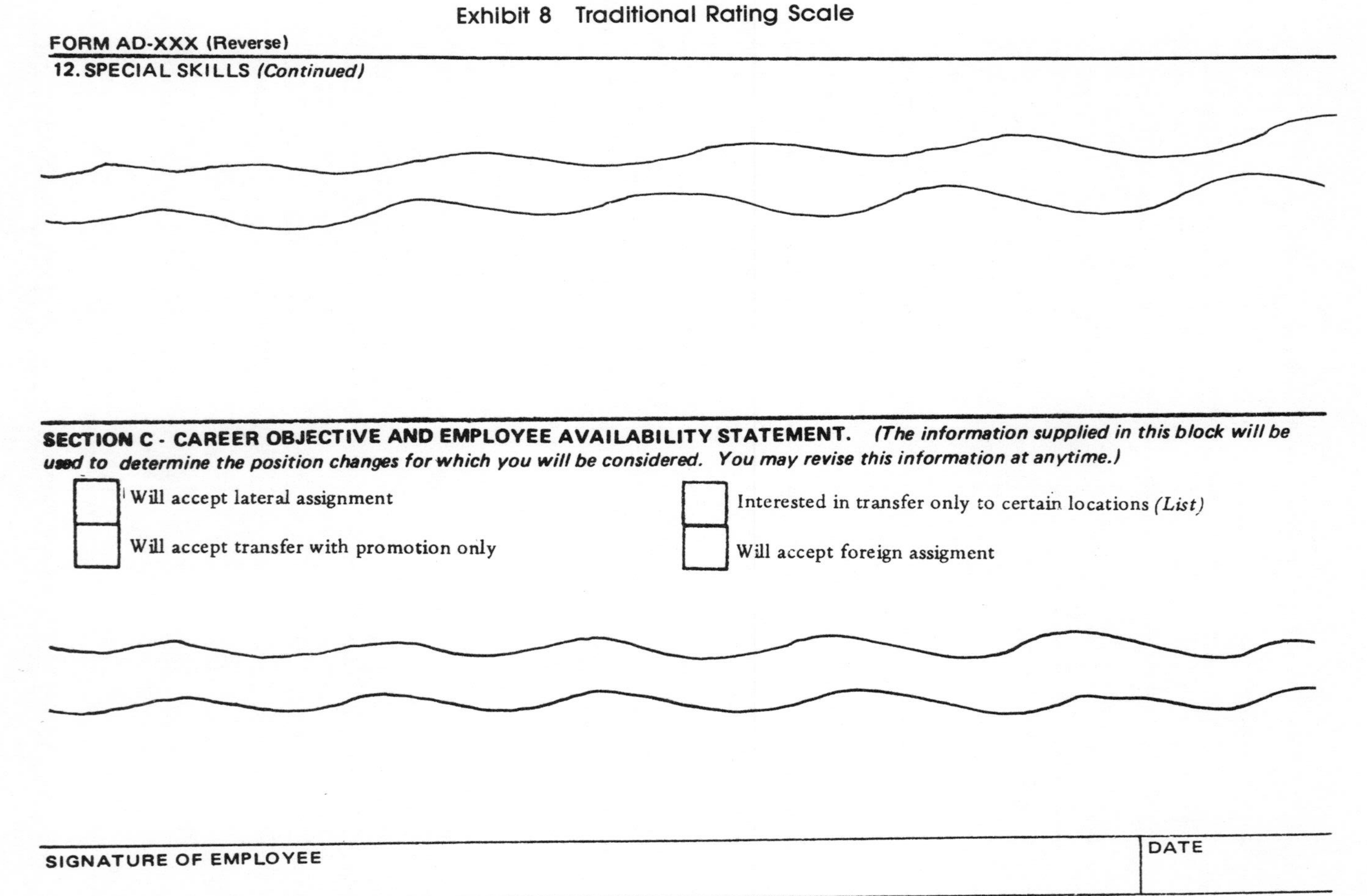

FORM AD-XXX (Reverse)

12. SPECIAL SKILLS *(Continued)*

SECTION C - CAREER OBJECTIVE AND EMPLOYEE AVAILABILITY STATEMENT. *(The information supplied in this block will be used to determine the position changes for which you will be considered. You may revise this information at anytime.)*

☐ Will accept lateral assignment

☐ Will accept transfer with promotion only

☐ Interested in transfer only to certain locations *(List)*

☐ Will accept foreign assigment

SIGNATURE OF EMPLOYEE	DATE

a typical global rating approach, the rater is asked to provide an overall estimate of performance without making distinctions among performance dimensions. The global rating often takes the form of a general category such as "Outstanding" or "Satisfactory." In the essay format, the rater is usually asked to respond narratively to a question such as "What is your overall evaluation of this individual's performance for the past year?" Although raters may provide information about strengths and weaknesses or accomplishments, the determination of performance dimensions is left totally unspecified, and the rater is given full discretion to infer what data are relevant or even included. In the case of a global essay and rating, very limited use can be made of the rating for administrative or feedback purposes, and, without specific performance criteria derived from a job analysis procedure, neither the global rating nor the general narrative can be considered job related, and each is therefore questionable as a legitimate measure from a legal perspective.

Strategy 2: Trait-rating scales Graphic- or trait-rating scales gathered momentum through the 1940s and still constitute one of the most common PA measurement approaches in use today (Lacho, Stearns, & Villere, 1979; Locher & Teel, 1977). Such scales are usually comprised of a list of personality traits, and the rater is asked to indicate on a numerical scale the degree to which the individual being appraised possesses these traits (Patten, 1977). Other variations ask the rater to evaluate an employee on each of several trait labels, with brief definitions, along a line containing a variety of adjectives (Landy & Farr, 1980). The trait-rating approach is multidimensional to the extent that some informal analysis is usually conducted to generate a limited number of traits appearing on the PA form (Schneier & Beatty, 1979). Exhibit 8 shows an example of a typical rating scale. The performance dimensions are usually very broadly defined as well as the levels within each dimension. Because they lack specific, job-related definitions, trait-rating scales are extremely vulnerable to errors such as halo, strictness, leniency, and central tendency that severely affect the validity, reliability, and discriminability of the ratings. Trait-rating scales have thus far not fared well in court in the presence of prima facie evidence of discrimination because of limited job relatedness and the absence of systematic job analysis procedures as a basis for the trait dimensions (Schneier & Beatty, 1979).

Few authors in the PA literature have come to the defense of personality traits as a basis for performance measurement. Although Kavanagh (1971) argued that existing evidence was insufficient to totally abandon use of trait-rating scales, Kane and Lawler (1979) summarized the more popular position in stating that "even though traits may relate in predictable ways to

Exhibit 9 A Ranking Procedure (See Blocks 51 and 52)

BUPERS USE ONLY

P1611-1

BUPERS USE ONLY

REPORT ON THE FITNESS OF OFFICERS

1. NAME (LAST, FIRST, MIDDLE): WATER, WALKER TREAD
2. GRADE: LT
3. DESIG.: 1105
4. SSN: 000-00-0002

5. ACDUTRA/TEMAC: X
6. UIC: 00000
7. SHIP/STATION: USS FOREVER SAIL (DLG 00)
8. DATE REPORTED: 74FEB10

OCCASION FOR REPORT: 9. PERIODIC; 10. DETACHMENT OF REPORTING SENIOR; 11. DETACHMENT OF OFFICER: X

PERIOD OF REPORT: 12. FROM: 74FEB10; 13. TO: 74FEB22

TYPE OF REPORT: 14. REGULAR: X

BASIS FOR OBSERVATION: 18. CLOSE: X; 19. FREQUENT; 20. INFREQUENT

21. EMPLOYMENT OF COMMAND (CONTINUED ON REVERSE SIDE OF RECORD COPY): EASTPAC LOCAL OPS
22. DAYS OF COMBAT: N

23. REPORTING SENIOR (LAST NAME, F.M.I.): EASY, I M
24. TITLE: CO
25. GRADE: CAPT
26. DESIG.: 1110
27. SSN: 000-00-0003

28. DUTIES ASSIGNED (CONTINUED ON REVERSE SIDE OF RECORD COPY): ACDUTRA, ASSISTANT OPS 1/2

ACTIVE DUTY FOR TRAINING DOES NOT REQUIRE SIX CHARACTER ABBREVIATION

SPECIFIC ASPECTS OF PERFORMANCE (TYPE IN OCR CODE LETTER FROM WORK SHEET)

Block	Code
29. GOAL SETTING & ACHIEVEMENT	N
30. SUBORDINATE MANAGEMENT & DEVELOPMENT	N
31. WORKING RELATIONS	B
32. EQUIP & MATERIAL MANAGE.	N
33. NAVY ORGAN. SUPPORT	B
34. RESPONSE IN STRESSFUL SITUATIONS	A
35. EQUAL OPPORTUNITY	B
36. SPEAKING ABILITY	A
37. WRITING ABILITY	N

WARFARE SPECIALTY SKILLS (FROM OCR WORK SHEET)

Block	Code
38. SEAMANSHIP	D
39. AIRMANSHIP	N
40. WATCH STANDING	B
41.	
42.	
43.	

A

44. SUBSPECIALTY CODE — REQUIRED BY BILLET: 45. YES; 46. NO — UTILIZATION: 47. FREQUENT; 48. INFREQUENT; 49. NONE — (WORK SHEET CODE) 50. PERFORMANCE: N

MISSION CONTRIBUTION	NOT OBS.	TOP 1%	5%	10%	30%	TYPICALLY EFFECTIVE OFFICER 50%	50%	BOTTOM 30%	MARG.	UNSAT *
51. EVALUATION				X						
52. SUMMARY	0	0	0	1	0	2	3	1	0	0

TREND OF PERFORMANCE: 53. FIRST REPORT: X; 54. CONSISTENT; 55. IMPROVING; 56. DECLINING *

RECORD COPY ONLY MUST BE INITIALLED.

B

DESIRABILITY (TYPE IN OCR CODE FROM WORK SHEET): 57. COMMAND: D; 58. OPERATIONAL: B; 59. STAFF: C; 60. JOINT/OSD: C; 61. FOREIGN SHORE: C

RECOMMENDATION FOR PROMOTION: 62. EARLY; 63. REGULAR: X; 64. NO *

RANKING FOR EARLY PROMOTION: 65. NUMBER RECOMMENDED: 0; 66. RANKING: N

PERSONAL TRAITS (TYPE IN OCR CODE FROM WORK SHEET)

Block	Code
67. JUDGMENT	A
68. IMAGINATION	C
69. ANALYTIC ABILITY	C
70. PERSONAL BEHAVIOR	BA
71. FORCEFULNESS	C
72. MILITARY BEARING	B

C

73. 74. 75. 76.

WEAKNESSES DISCUSSED? 77. NONE NOTED: X; 78. YES; 79. NO *

STATEMENT: 80. NOT DESIRED: N; 81. ATTACHED: N

ACCEPTABLE PROCEDURE WHEN IMPRACTICABLE TO OBTAIN SIGNATURE.

D

82. SIGNATURE OF OFFICER EVALUATED (IAW BUPERS INST. 1611-12-SERIES) "I ACKNOWLEDGE THAT I HAVE SEEN THIS REPORT AND HAVE BEEN APPRISED OF MY PERFORMANCE."

COPY FORWARDED

SIGNATURE MUST ALSO APPEAR ON RECORD COPY.

E

83. DATE FORWARDED: 74FEB25
84.

85. SIGNATURE OF REPORTING SENIOR: I M Easy

F

86. DATE FORWARDED

87. SIGNATURE OF REGULAR REPORTING SENIOR ON CONCURRENT AND CONCURRENT/SPECIAL REPORT

NAVPERS 1611/1 (REV. 9-72) S/N 0106-078-3113

OCR COPY (0-73)

6 FIGURE A ENCLOSURE (2)

more nearly ultimate criteria of performance, this no more qualifies them as surrogates for such criteria than it qualifies IQ scores as surrogates for school grades" (p. 445).

Evaluating performance using trait-rating scales requires a great deal of rigorous inference by the rater to make appropriate connections between specific behaviors observed and the appropriate general rating dimensions. Further, trait ratings are difficult to use in PA feedback sessions where discussions focused on improving "loyalty" or "attitude" become awkward and uncomfortable.

Strategy 3: Ranking procedures Although they have received only limited treatment in PA literature (Cummings & Schwab, 1973; Patten, 1977), ranking procedures are still found in PA practice. Exhibit 9 contains one example of a ranking procedure (see Block 51). In such a procedure, the rater is asked to provide an overall evaluation of performance by checking one of the following categories: Top 1%, Top 3%, Top 5%, Top 10%, Top 30%, Top 50% (Typical), Bottom 30%, Marginal, and Unsatisfactory. In other ranking procedures, raters are asked to distribute their employees along a scale on the basis of performance or simply to list employees' names in order of effectiveness on particular dimensions.

In ranking situations, the ratings are indirect, and the rater is given great latitude to infer what distinguishes levels of effective performance. Although ranking procedures often show reasonable interrater reliability and eliminate other rating errors such as central tendency, they are typically not based on specifically defined measures of job-relevant performance and are thus very vulnerable to legal difficulties. Also, performance feedback sessions using such rankings are difficult to conduct, since raters must struggle to explain why employees compare with each other as ranked. However, ranking is probably the most comparative of all approaches because employee performance is rated purely in terms of the performance of others.

Strategy 4: Critical Incident Methods Although only rarely used today, the critical incident method is one of the earlier attempts to move away from trait-rating approaches (Flanagan, 1954). The critical incident method requires the rater to document positive and negative behavioral events that have occurred during a given performance period. The intent is to use this information to review performance as a series of "go" and "no-go" behaviors related to a job (Patten, 1977). Besides emphasizing the importance of observation and recording, this approach requires a great degree of rater inference to determine which incidents are critical to job performance. Also, other techniques—such as trait-rating scales or global evaluations—are often used in conjunction with the critical incidents to summarize and quantify job performance. This approach is subject to all the shortcomings previously cited.

Strategy 5: Behaviorally Based Scales and BARS Behaviorally based scales represent a significant movement beyond global and trait ratings. Typically, behavioral scales are based on some form of job analysis to determine what behaviors and, subsequently, what behavioral dimensions actually constitute job performance. The behaviors, specifically defined, become the anchors for rating scales. Whereas these scales more likely represent job-relevant dimensions of performance, they still pose problems for the rater in determining which actually observed behaviors match with specifically anchored performance levels. Despite this difficulty, several researchers have recommended the use of the scales (Barrett, 1966; Campbell et al., 1970), since they require less inference on the part of the rater than traditional trait-rating approaches.

Smith and Kendall (1963) made a major refinement in behavioral scaling techniques by creating a procedure to measure performance in multidimensional, behaviorally specific terms known as BARS. The BARS procedure, with minor variations, typically involves five steps (Schwab, Heneman, & DeCotiis, 1975):

1 ***Critical incidents.*** Individuals who are knowledgeable of the job in question (incumbents and supervisors) describe specific examples of both effective and ineffective job behaviors.
2 ***Performance dimensions.*** The behavioral incidents are clustered into a smaller set of performance dimensions (usually five to 10).
3 ***Retranslation.*** Another group of job-knowledgeable participants assigns each incident to the dimension that best describes it. Those incidents meeting some predetermined percentage of agreement with the group in Step 2 regarding placement (typically 50–80%) are considered to be "retranslated."
4 ***Scaling incidents.*** The same group as in Step 3 rates the behavior described in each incident in terms of effectiveness or ineffectiveness on the appropriate dimension by typically using seven- or nine-point scales. Average effectiveness ratings for each incident are then determined and a standard deviation criterion (typically s.d. $\leq$ 1.50 for a seven-point scale) is set for determining which incidents will be included in the final anchored scales.
5 ***Final instrument.*** A subset of the incidents that meets both the retranslation and s.d. criterion is used as a behavioral anchor for the final performance dimensions. A final BARS instrument typically is

Exhibit 10 Typical Scale from BARS Procedure*

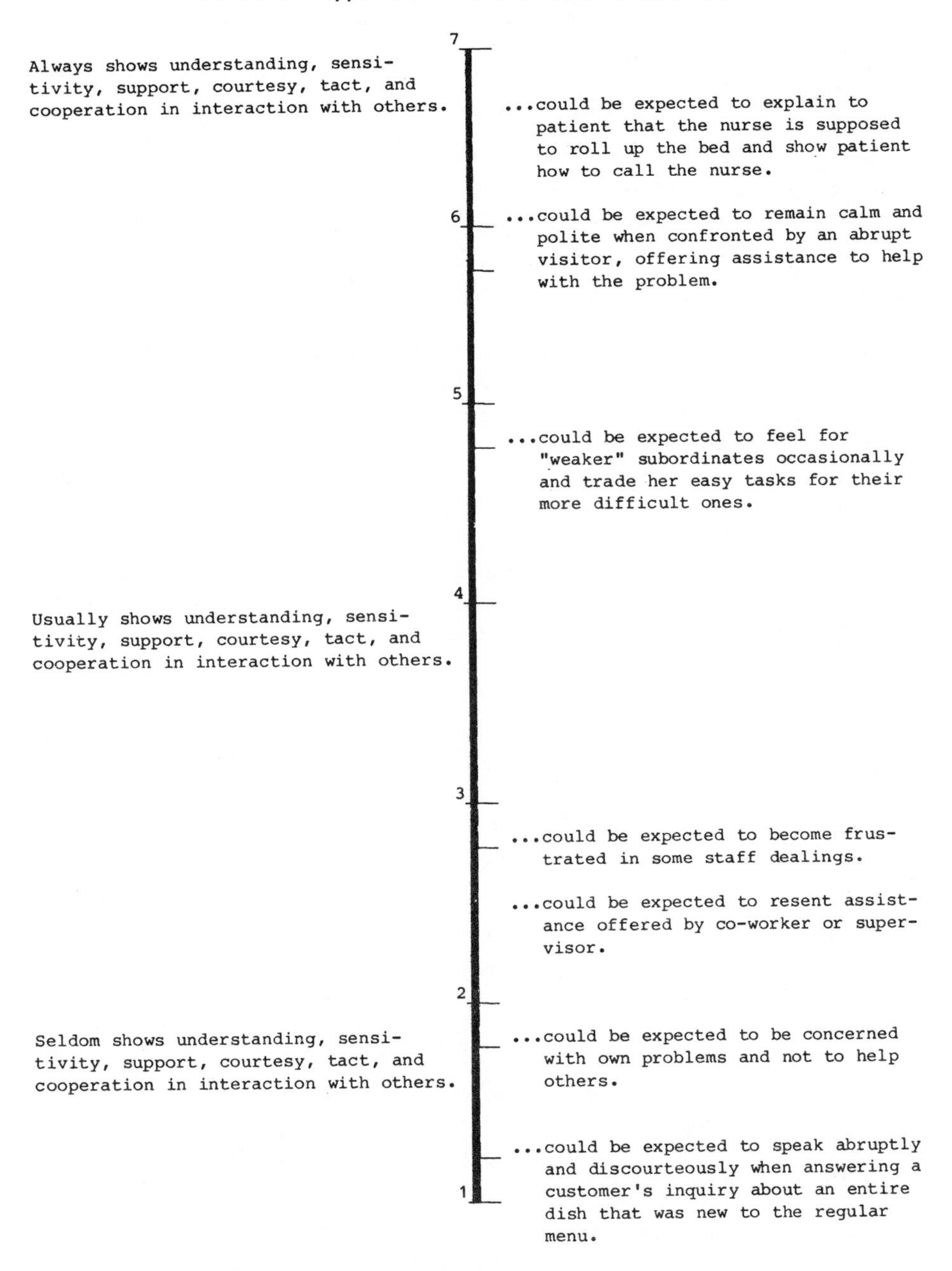

*Hamner, W. C. & Schmidt, F. L. (Eds.). *Contemporary Problems* in *Personnel* (Rev. ed.). Chicago: St. Clair, 1977, printed with permission.

comprised of a series of vertical scales (one scale per dimension) that are anchored by the included incidents. Each incident is placed on the scales based on the rating determined in Step 4.*

Exhibit 10 contains a sample BARS for the dimension "forming and maintaining interpersonal relationships," developed for nurses in hospitals (cf., Goodale, 1977). From this example, it is clear that performance dimensions are more clearly defined and based on more observable behaviors. The rater, however, is still required to make inferences about behavior, since a specific set of behavioral anchors may not exactly match behaviors observed on the job. Thus the rater must look for similarities and differences between one set of behaviors (job observed) and those presented as anchors for each performance dimension.

Despite the rigor required for BARS procedures, there is evidence that this approach does not necessarily contribute to increased reliability, reduction in leniency effects (Schwab, Heneman, & DeCotiis, 1975), or enhanced independence of dimensions (Arvey & Hoyle, 1974; Borman & Vallon, 1974). In fact, several authors have suggested that a lack of rigor in the selection and scaling of anchors creates the same vulnerability to traditional rating errors as trait-rating scales (Bernardin, 1977; Landy & Farr, 1980; Schwab, Heneman, & DeCotiis, 1975).

BARS does appear to create measures based on a systematic analysis of job requirements. This behaviorally based procedure and its variations, such as behavioral expectation scales (BES) and behavioral observation scales, do result in specific job-relevant performance dimensions and are commonly considered to be potentially legally defensible as selection procedures.

Strategy 6: Objective and Goal-Setting Procedures Whereas behaviorally based scales focus on job behaviors, objective and goal-setting procedures focus on outcomes—what the employee produces as a result of job performance. These approaches—MBO (Odiorne, 1965), goal setting (Locke, 1968), or work planning and review (Meyer, Kay, & French, 1965)—view job performance as a multidimensional series of expected results that can be compared with actual performance results. Typically, goals and standards are set either by the manager alone or jointly by the manager and employee. Evaluation is based on whether the goals or objectives are met in relation to the predetermined standards.

According to McConkie (1979), "goals and objectives . . . are specific, measurable, time bounded, and joined to an action plan" (p. 37) The Corporate form shown in Exhibit 11 includes an MBO procedure (see pages

*D.L. Schwab, H.G. Heneman, & T.A. DeCotiis, "Behaviorally Anchored Rating Scales: A Review of the Literature," *Personnel Psychology,* 1975, pp. 550-551.

IBM

Performance Planning, Counseling & Evaluation

IBM Confidential

Employee Name (Last, First and Initial)		Employee Serial
Position Title	Position Code - 4 Digit	Date Assigned Present Position
Date Assigned To This Appraiser	Date of Performance Plan	Date of Performance Evaluation
Location	Office or Dept. Number	Division

ZMO4-6715-6 (Rev. 1/77)

Exhibit 11 An MBO Form

IBM Confidential
PERFORMANCE PLANNING

RESPONSIBILITIES (Key words to describe the major elements of this employee's job.)	**PERFORMANCE FACTORS AND/OR RESULTS TO BE ACHIEVED** (A more specific statement of the employee's key responsibilities and/or goals employee can reasonably be expected to achieve in the coming period.)	**RELATIVE IMPORTANCE**

CHANGES IN PERFORMANCE PLAN (May be recorded anytime during the appraisal period.)

OPTIONAL ADDITIONAL PLANS (Where considered appropriate by manager and employee.)

Exhibit 11 (Continued)

IBM Confidential

PERFORMANCE EVALUATION

ACTUAL ACHIEVEMENTS	LEVEL OF ACHIEVEMENT	Far Exceeded	Consistently Exceeded	Exceeded	Consistently Met	Did Not Meet

CONTINUING RESPONSIBILITIES

(Responsibilities, not covered at left, to be considered only when they have had a significant positive or negative effect on the overall performance.)

RELATIONSHIPS WITH OTHERS (JOB RELATED)

(Significant positive or negative influence this employee has had on the performance of other IBM employees.)

ADDITIONAL SIGNIFICANT ACCOMPLISHMENTS

OVERALL RATING

(Considering all factors, check the definition which best describes this employee's overall performance during the past period.

Satisfactory

- ☐ Results achieved **far exceeded** the requirements of the job **in all areas.**
- ☐ Results achieved **consistently exceeded** the requirements of the job **in all key areas.**
- ☐ Results achieved **consistently met** the requirements of the job **and exceeded the requirements in many areas.**
- ☐ Results achieved **consistently met** the requirements of the job.

Unsatisfactory

- ☐ Results achieved **did not meet** the requirements of the job.

Exhibit 11 (Continued)

IBM Confidential

Counseling Summary

Employee Strengths	Suggested Improvements
1. ________	1. ________
2. ________	2. ________
3. ________	3. ________

Significant Interview Comments

(Record here only those additional significant items brought up during the discussion by either you or the employee which are not recorded elsewhere in this document.)

Manager's Signature	Print Name	Date of Interview

Employee Review

Optional Comments: If the employee wishes to do so, any comments concerning the performance plan or evaluation (for example, agreement or disagreement) may be indicated in the space provided below.

I have reviewed this document and discussed the contents with my manager. My signature means that I have been advised of my performance status and does not necessarily imply that I agree with this evaluation.

Employee's Signature | Date

Management Review

Optional Comments

Reviewer's Signature | Print Name | Date

50, 51). The rater determines not only which aspects of performance to measure but also which standards to use in determining goal achievement. Thus, depending on the nature of the job to be analyzed, goal-setting approaches may require a high degree of both job analysis and inferential skills to be done effectively. Further, goal accomplishment is often influenced by factors outside an employee's control, and the responsibility for the lack of goal completion may be difficult to establish (Goodale, 1977).

A review of goal-setting studies by Latham and Yukl (1975) provides evidence for performance improvement when goals are specific, difficult, and accepted, but the feasibility of goal-setting approaches for complex jobs has been questioned. Levinson (1970) discovered a tendency for objective-setting measures to result in disregard for less quantifiable aspects of job performance. Schneier and Beatty (1979) note that managerial jobs are often measured in terms of unit, rather than individual, objectives. Levinson (1970) has questioned the degree to which an individual can be held accountable for outcomes requiring interdependent employee efforts. Although goal-setting procedures have not been directly tested in court, they do appear to be job relevant. The degree to which job representativeness is distorted in goal-setting procedures has not yet been determined but would appear to be significant.

Strategy 7: Organizational Records Smith (1976) has noted that organizations regularly collect considerable amounts of "hard" data for purposes other than PA measurement. Data such as production rates and cost variances may constitute job-relevant and objective performance measures requiring little inference by raters. In addition, personnel information such as accident and absence rates, although applicable to a limited percentage of employees, is potentially available as objective performance measures. Unfortunately, it is difficult to obtain objective measures for most jobs (Landy & Farr, 1980). Also, many objective measures may relate more to unit than to individual performance, resulting in an ambiguous relationship between individual job performance and objective performance criteria.

EVALUATING THE EFFECTIVENESS OF PERFORMANCE MEASUREMENT APPROACHES

It is helpful to apply the evaluation criteria cited previously (content validity and job relevance, criterion or construct validity, reliability, discriminability, and usefulness) to each of these seven performance measurement strategies. For some of the strategies (particularly BARS), the criteria have been extensively examined in the literature, whereas no empirical tests have been conducted for others.

Examining which of the seven performance measurement strategies meet which criteria yields the following trends. The approaches requiring highly inferential judgments (such as essays, rankings, or trait ratings) have been found to be wanting on criteria such as validity, reliability or even discriminability. What has kept these methods in use is their relative ease in making judgments that can be used in a series of administrative choices (for example, ranking employees to distribute merit pay).

Overall, the BARS approach (and its variations) and the Objective and Goal-Setting approach show the strongest relative profiles using these criteria. Both methods focus on dimensions of performance designed to be job-related. BARS shows a unique strength in providing data useful for administrative purposes. In contrast, the highly individualized aspects of many objective and goal-setting approaches create difficulty in generating the comparative data needed for many administrative decisions but are useful for performance planning and feedback.

It is important to note that even these two measurement approaches received only moderate support from the literature. One may be tempted to conclude from these data that no measurement approach is very workable. However, such a conclusion is premature and probably inaccurate. The next chapter cites evidence indicating that the rater and the ratee often have much more impact on the effectiveness of PA approaches than any measurement format itself. In essence, PA measurement approaches, like any other tools, do vary in quality, but the effectiveness of these approaches is predominantly determined by who uses them and how they are used.

In Chapter 5 we thoroughly evaluate both BARS and Objective vs. Goal-Setting measurement approaches by looking at their validity and usefulness when incorporated into an ongoing PA system. Determining whether these measurement strategies work requires evidence based not on abstract judgments made of fictional employees but rather on their effectiveness as part of a PA system in actual use.

IN CONCLUSION

Having reviewed the psychometric complexities of performance and performance measurement and examined the effectiveness of existing measurement approaches, the reader may be bewildered and even more frustrated than before. Why has so much effort been invested in developing more effective measurement strategies that have so little payoff for organizations? And, more important, where do we go from here?

The following conclusions help explain why much of the measurement research has been less than helpful in a practical sense and point out issues that warrant attention in designing and using performance measurement systems.

There is no universally best way to measure performance PA data can be expected to serve many different functions, and no one technique is always acceptable. The reasons for appraising performance determine what aspects of performance need to be measured. What is measured, in turn, dictates the appropriate technique for capturing performance data. Thus it is extremely important that PA designers and users clearly understand what purposes the PA system must serve.

Organizations need to more systematically define what is meant by job performance Organizations have spent too little time defining performance criteria. Measurement approaches based on some variety of formal, systematic job analysis, although initially costly and time consuming, pay off by providing more relevant, valid, reliable, and usable performance measures. No measurement approach can compensate for vague performance criteria.

Behavior-based (BARS) and outcome-based (goal-setting) approaches are superior to trait-rating approaches As stated previously, an initial hurdle in performance measurement is to identify specific, measurable and relevant performance criteria. Traditional trait approaches use general, ambiguous performance criteria that result in tremendous inaccuracy and irrelevance of PA ratings. Behavioral and outcome-based approaches define performance criteria in more systematic and concrete terms, providing less room for error and more meaningful data for decision making and employee feedback.

Performance measurement, in practice, is more ratable than measurable As noted previously, very few purely objective measures exist for most jobs, and most performance data are based on ratings or judgments about job performance. Managers, or others functioning as raters, can significantly affect the validity and reliability of rating data generated by any measurement technique. Although no human being can ever be "objective," organizations can prepare raters to make more systematic and accurate judgments.

THE BOTTOM LINE

This chapter has reviewed some of the most elusive and abstract parts of

PA—*what* we mean by performance and *how* we ask the manager to observe and evaluate it. The chapter raises issues that we often overlook in designing PA systems. They are as follows.

The vagaries of defining effective performance In looking at PA systems, the ones that have the greatest clarity (e.g., MBO) may be the ones which select a narrow subset of what we mean by effective performance. PA systems that one way or another incorporate traits, behaviors, and outcomes more directly address what a person brings to the job, what the person does, and how well he/she succeeds. Any systems that look exclusively at only one of these three aspects of performance is to be distrusted.

Legal guidelines: A PA handbook The court cases and federal guidelines around Title VII give you some remarkably specific suggestions for *(a)* what your PA system should measure and how, *(b)* what you should do to check if your PA system is fair and useful, and *(c)* how the PA system should be administered. These guidelines have value above and beyond their keeping you out of court.

Performance measurement: Enjoy the diversity We shared with you seven of the more prominent strategies for capturing a person's performance. We purposely avoided telling you which ones to avoid. In fact, all have some value; some are just better suited to meeting the wide range of criteria than others. What this list can give you is a way to categorize approaches currently used in your organization and to look for strengths and weaknesses of these in light of other possibilities.

4

The Human Context of Performance Appraisal

The world is full of obvious things which nobody by any chance observes. (Attributed to Sherlock Holmes in *Hound of the Baskervilles,* Doyle, 1968, p. 30)

Item: Surveys show that up to 93% of PA programs ask an employee's immediate supervisor to take sole responsibility for doing the appraisal (Lacho, Stearns, & Villere, 1979). The manager is the driving force in most appraisals.

Item: A typical manager has limited contact with his/her employees. Recent studies of how managers actually behave show that managers spend only 5–10% of their workweek with any one subordinate. These contacts are in a limited range of settings, often formal meetings (see, e.g., McCall, Morrison, & Hannan, 1978). Clearly, managers have direct access to only a small and possibly unrepresentative sample of their employees' work.

Item: Managers often do a cursory job when giving PA feedback. A survey conducted by the authors of professional and managerial employees in a high-technology corporation revealed that only 28% reported that their PA discussion lasted an hour or more. Only 16% of the respondents was ever involved in a follow-up meeting to discuss issues that came up during the PA discussion. And only 24% reported knowing the evaluation criteria prior to the PA session. PA often gets shortchanged by the individual most critical to the process—the manager giving the appraisal—and those most affected—the appraisees—know it.

PA typically involves two principals—the appraiser and the appraisee—and two major aspects—measurement and feedback. Traditionally, the immediate supervisor has appraised the employee by completing an evaluation form and giving some performance information to the employee in a private discussion. As legal guidelines for personnel practices have gained prominence and day-to-day management of employee groups has become increasingly complex, traditional supervisor–employee PA practices have been called into question.

This chapter approaches PA not from the technological and legal vantage points but the human side of the PA enterprise. Chapter 3 treated the manager as appraiser rather like an instrument, perhaps the combination of a high-powered microscope (to observe employees' performance) and a space-age computer (to process these data). The employee as appraisee, in turn, was treated as the object of the measurement process, that is, the performer whose traits, behaviors, and accomplishments were put under this microscope and processed through the computer.

One is reminded of the long-standing observation that organizations would work well if only there were no people involved to confuse matters. Whereas the psychometric framework of PA emphasizes the need for objectivity, it also grudgingly acknowledges the inevitability of retaining a certain degree of error or subjectivity in the measurement process. The position taken in this chapter is that subjectivity is more than error; subjectivity is also the recognition that people are not only rational and fallible but also are responsive to real and perceived pressures in PA. Emphasis is placed on understanding how the roles of appraiser and appraisee impact the interactions and outcomes of PA.

The chapter explores this human context of PA by examining the following:

1 The limits of the immediate supervisor ratings.
2 Alternative rating sources.
3 Advantages and disadvantages of multiple raters.
4 How ratee characteristics affect performance measurement.
5 The usefulness of typical information as performance feedback.
6 Employee participation as an integral part of the PA process.

WHO RATES?

Supervisory Ratings

Traditionally, "supervisory ratings of performance" and "performance appraisal" have been virtually synonymous terms. Lacho, Stearns, and

Villere (1979), for example, found that the supervisor was the only appraiser in 78–93% of the programs surveyed. Surveys have shown that the supervisor participates in the employee's appraisal (not necessarily as the only appraiser) in 78–100% of the appraisal systems studied (Feild & Holley, 1977; Holley, Feild, & Barnett, 1976; Lacho, Stearns, & Villere, 1979; Lazer & Wikstrom, 1977; Locher & Teel, 1977). The manager, responsible for making administrative decisions that affect his/her direct subordinates, has been seen as the most appropriate person to make performance judgments on which to base these decisions.

Some authors and several recent court cases, however, have challenged this traditional PA approach and have pointed out some problems with the immediate supervisor being the sole appraiser. These problems have been shown to limit the accuracy and usefulness of performance ratings.

First, the manager may not be in the best position to assess an employee's performance. Physical distance from the employee, unfamiliarity with the job requirements or duties, or lack of opportunities to observe the employee at work can result in inaccurate performance ratings. The courts, in particular, have emphasized the need for raters to maintain sufficient employee contact and observation to be able to rate accurately (Odom, 1979). In general, research on the amount and type of contact between rater and ratee shows that relevancy of contact is more important than mere frequency, particularly if regular contact bears no relationship to selected performance dimensions (Landy & Guion, 1970; Landy & Farr, 1980).

Second, the manager may be interested only in certain aspects of the employee's performance such as technical knowledge or dependability and overlook other performance factors such as supervisory or interpersonal skills. That is, the perspective of the supervisor may distort or narrow the performance picture, limiting its usefulness for employee development and improvement.

Third, and perhaps most significant, it is fairly common for managers first to make administrative decisions (regarding salary increases, promotions, etc.) and then manipulate the performance ratings to correspond with those decisions (see, e.g., Warmke & Billings, 1979; Teel, 1980). Thus an inverse relationship may exist, with appraisal being used to justify personnel decisions after the fact.

Because PA systems are often viewed as falling short of their goals, the manager's central role in PA has received close scrutiny. Explanations for the incompetence of managers at conducting PA include inadequate cognitive ability, lack of training, and role conflict (see, e.g., Bernardin & Walter, 1977; Schneier, 1977b). These and other problems have been recognized by managers and behavioral scientists alike, and attempts have been made to solve them. Incentive for these attempts has also come from

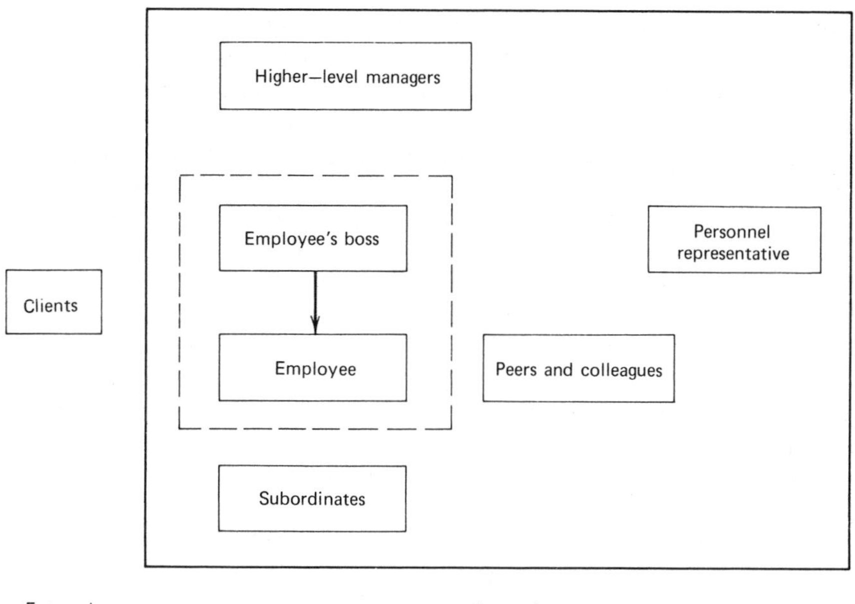

Figure 3 Potential appraisal sources.

the courts, since the validity of supervisory ratings as "true" performance criteria has been questioned in legal proceedings.

Alternative Raters

One obvious solution to the problems just cited is to find a different appraiser (or set of appraisers) who is willing and able to rate an employee's performance more accurately than the immediate supervisor. The search for alternative raters has resulted in some research findings on the motivation and abilities of different performance raters, including the employees themselves, peers, subordinates, higher-level managers, and personnel staff members.

Figure 3 illustrates an obvious, yet critical, fact. All employees have multiple relationships. The most critical one is usually with the immediate supervisor, and, as the dotted line in the figure indicates, PA occurs within that relationship. However, an employee may also work with peers, clients (either inside or outside the organization), and higher-level managers (sometimes directly and often through the immediate manager). If an employee has supervisory responsibilities, the subordinates may know a great deal about the employee's performance. Beyond this, an employee may have strong relationships with others outside the organization, such as clients or customers, who can both affect and understand the employee's performance.

There are signs that organizations are beginning to involve others besides the supervisor in the appraisal process. Recent surveys show that self-ratings are used in 5–14% of the PA programs sampled, and 2–5% uses a personnel representative's ratings (Lazer & Wikstrom, 1977; Locher & Teel, 1977). Although these surveys show virtually no programs in which peer or subordinate ratings are used, there are cases where these occur in some form. For example, Gulf Oil is experimenting with a top-management appraisal system that includes self-ratings and ratings by managers, peers, and subordinates (Bush & Stinson, 1980).

Points of Comparison

There is evidence that when groups of raters in different organizational positions relative to an employee rate performance the resulting correlations are only low to moderate (Baird, 1977; Holzbach, 1978; Landy & Farr, 1980; Lawler, 1967; Prien & Liske, 1962; Schneier & Beatty, 1978; Thornton, 1968). However, studies which have compared different rater groups (supervisors, peers, self, subordinates) have found few explanations that consistently account for these correlations. For example, studies comparing supervisory and peer ratings have generally found peers to be more lenient raters than supervisors (Miner, 1968; Rothaus, Morton, & Hanson, 1965; Schneier, 1977b; Zedeck et al., 1974). On the other hand, studies of these two rater groups have shown that neither group consistently has better interrater reliability (Gordon & Medland, 1965; Klieger & Mosel, 1953).

In studies comparing supervisory and self-ratings, self-ratings have been found to be both more lenient (Kirchner, 1965; Parker et al., 1959) and harsher (Heneman, 1974). Thornton (1968) reviewed the literature on self-appraisal and concluded that self-ratings generally tend to show more leniency, less discriminant validity, less reliability, less agreement with other sources, and less halo than others' ratings (supervisor, peers, and subordinates), although other reviews have found less definitive trends (Landy & Farr, 1980).

In studies comparing supervisory ratings, peer ratings, and self-ratings simultaneously, some evidence indicates supervisory and peer ratings have more convergent and discriminant validity than self-ratings (Lawler, 1967). Some rating differences may be a result of (*a*) disagreements among raters on what behaviors are required to perform well or which criteria are most important, (*b*) different sources of bias, and (*c*) different bases for both collecting and using performance information, resulting from differences in ability and opportunity to rate.

Some evidence demonstrates that different raters attach importance to different performance factors or criteria. An employee's manager, for example, appears to consider the technical aspects of work, or job knowledge, to be an important performance criterion, as well as initiative and dependability (Miner, 1968; Sanders & Peay, 1975; Schneier, 1977b). Peers, perhaps because they spend more time with employees, seem to weigh interpersonal skills heavily, as do the employees themselves (Levinson, 1972; Sanders & Peay, 1975; Schneier, 1977b). Borman and Vallon (1974) and Landy et al. (1976) found that peers and supervisors actually generated different performance dimensions for the same job in the process of developing behaviorally anchored scales. These different perspectives can cloud the performance dimensions used in appraisal, particularly if they are general. For example, "quality (or quantity) of work" can be interpreted differently, depending on what is considered important by the appraiser.

Different rater groups are also motivated by different sources of bias. For example, the supervisor may rate primarily because administrative decisions and distribution of rewards must be justified by performance ratings of subordinates (Sanders & Peay, 1975). The supervisor, however, must also consider that exceptionally high ratings may encourage employees to exert pressure on the supervisor for unavailable salary increases (see, e.g., Schneier & Beatty, 1978). Further, there is reason to believe the manager may rate less leniently because of some rivalry with subordinates and the need to feel more competent (Levinson, 1972).

Peers may also feel some rivalry with their colleagues, but peers may rate more leniently because of mutual respect, attraction, and a sense of togetherness. Employees themselves are motivated to get the highest ratings possible, since PA ratings have personal consequences in the present and future (Levinson, 1972; Schneier, 1977b).

Different rater groups may be influenced not only by their biases and perspectives but also by their ability to rate performance accurately. Organizational positions, for example, may be connected with ability to rate, because peers or subordinates may have more relevant (and frequent) opportunities to observe the employee than does the supervisor. In "management by exception" settings, employees may not have much contact with their supervisors, except when problems arise. Managers who observe subordinates mainly in problem-oriented or stress-producing situations may retain negative views of employee performance (Lewis & Taylor, 1955). Overall, however, these biases may help explain why different groups of raters rate performance level differently.

DeCotiis and Petit (1978) reported several factors that seem to affect rater group accuracy. For example, when ratings are more confidential and less publicly observable, accuracy is increased. Thus DeCotiis and Petit concluded supervisory ratings may be less accurate because they have a lower probability of remaining confidential (the employee will probably at least sign the completed PA form) than peer ratings (that are typically averaged to maintain peer confidentiality).

Accuracy may also vary as a function of accountability. Both the supervisor and the employee are held more accountable for the ratings than peers or other observers. From their comparison of confidentiality, accountability, and several other factors, DeCotiis and Petit (1978) concluded that the supervisor is potentially the most accurate rater, followed by the employee, and then his/her peers. Subordinates of employees and personnel representatives did not fare well in this analysis.

The question of whose ratings are more accurate is difficult to answer, because absolute measures of performance do not exist for most jobs. It is possible, as Dunnette and Borman (1979) have pointed out, that ratings made from different perspectives are equally valid. This viewpoint has been supported by other work (Landy & Farr, 1980).

There are undoubtedly relevant rater group factors other than those presented here, and all these factors are subject to individual as well as group differences. Overall, however, these factors may help explain why different groups of raters rate performance level differently.

Who, Then, Should Rate?

The conclusion from the previous analyses is that no single performance rater is better than the employee's immediate supervisor. Using ratings from an alternate rating source would provide a different perspective on performance evaluation, but it is not clear that another's perspective is more valid or that others could provide their perspective with less bias or error. Thus, whereas a different rater may solve some appraisal problems, other problems either remain or are created.

There is, however, the option of using multiple raters. The idea here is to capture several perspectives on an employee's performance so that a larger number of important performance factors are reviewed and the overall ratings are more accurate (less susceptible to all individual or rater group biases). Miner (1968) reported that army studies have shown the average of several persons' ratings to be superior to one rater's appraisal.

Any rater's judgments are limited, and this fact argues for involving more than one rater. As Schneier (1977b) suggested, PA can be improved by getting judgments from several sources, particularly those representing different groups. Many managers already do this informally. For example, it is not unusual for the manager of a salesperson to "sound out" a few of the employee's clients at PA time. Structuring such additional evaluations by managers, and keeping control of the process in the manager's hands, may be a valuable addition to formal PA systems. Using additional raters (even if only for feedback information purposes) makes sense, particularly in organizations using a matrix structure in which an employee may be formally reporting to one manager but spending the majority of his/her time on projects led by other managers. In such cases multiple raters may be required to get a complete picture of the employee.

Schneier (1977b) cites five potential advantages of using raters from different groups in the appraisal process:

1 It generates a larger data base on which personnel decisions can be made.
2 It helps identify extremely biased or different ratings.
3 It allows appraisal from multiple perspectives.
4 It permits assessment of the reliability of ratings as well as the sensitivity of the rating format.
5 It allows participation by others besides superiors in the appraisal process that can foster commitment to the system.

One general caution which must be considered is that any two raters will disagree. Borman (1978) conducted a critical study in which several raters observed a fictional employee under "ideal circumstances." That is, all raters had a thorough understanding of what was desired and an equal exposure to the employee's behavior. Even here, highly trained raters disagreed on how well individuals performed. Borman attributed this to the highly complex, multistage process of (*a*) observing, (*b*) evaluating, and (*c*) weighting those evaluations to come up with an overall rating. According to Borman, using several raters creates a more complex picture of the employee's performance, one that reflects more accurately the organizational reality in which the employee finds himself/herself.

There are also other caveats to consider before adopting a multiple rater approach:

1 Combining or averaging appraisal ratings can mask the differences that come from various perspectives. The information provided by "pure" ratings is lost (Schneier, 1977b).
2 Given that rater group divergences are expected, it is difficult to tell which differences are due to perspective and which to bias. That is, differences in ratings may be valid or erroneous (Schneier, 1977b).

3 Individual raters may feel less accountable for the appraisal in a multiple rater system, and the accuracy of the ratings by individual raters may decrease (DeCotiis & Petit, 1977).
4 Someone must give the employee feedback on the ratings, and interpreting ratings made by others can be difficult and inaccurate.
5 Using multiple raters, particularly from nontraditional sources, is a costly venture. By supplementing (not replacing) managerial ratings with others, the cost in staff time easily skyrockets. The literature in no way addresses the issue of the relative return on that investment. Some articles (e.g., Kane & Lawler, 1978) allude to certain problems in user reaction when one gets ratings from nontraditional sources.

Whether multiple or alternative rating approaches begin to flourish, it is virtually a certainty that the manager, as the employee's immediate supervisor, will continue to be the major rating source. As such, working to correct the manager's rating biases will become an even more important and fruitful approach. Some encouraging research in the area by Bernardin and Walter (1977) (see Chapter 6) indicates that training managers to avoid biases (such as halo effect) has a substantial and long-standing impact on the quality of ratings.

One other perspective on the validity of supervisory ratings has long been overlooked. Perhaps the bias or subjectivity of the manager's ratings is inevitable given the high stakes. One issue unfortunately left unexplored in the PA literature is whether the error, particularly in the form of leniency in rating low levels of performance, is due to the substantial consequences often attached to the rating. One suspects that most managers who realize that their employee's salary increase depends on satisfactory PA ratings are likely to give their employee the benefit of the doubt. We need to understand better the impact of attaching such rewards to the PA ratings—do they make honest appraisals of employees such as "marginal performers" a psychological impossibility?

WHO IS RATED?

Appraisal ratings are also affected by the characteristics and positions of employees being appraised. The level and uniqueness of the employee's position, the employee's physical and personality traits, and the employee's level of performance appear to have an impact on performance ratings.

Position Differences

Recent survey results show that some job groupings are more often included under a formal appraisal program than others. Employee groups most frequently appraised are professional and technical workers, first-level supervisors, office employees, and middle management; more than 70% of lower and middle levels of management are covered by a PA system (Lazer & Wikstrom, 1977). Formal appraisals are typically given to these white-collar employees by their immediate supervisor in both a written and verbal form; these appraisals are normally reviewed by the supervisor's manager (Lazer & Wikstrom, 1977).

Appraisal of higher-level managers tends to follow a different pattern (Lazer & Wikstrom, 1977). Only an average of 55% of the organizations surveyed includes top-level managers in a formal PA system. Appraisals at this level are most often conducted by the manager's immediate supervisor, although not as frequently as in other levels (86% compared with 95%); they are more likely to be conducted by a group or committee (9% versus 4–5% at lower levels).

Higher-level positions are more difficult to appraise for several reasons. These jobs are characterized by uncertainty, long-term and sometimes intangible goals, and little written documentation (see McCall, Morrison, & Hannan, 1978). Also, executives typically spend more time with people outside the organization, making appraisal of their behavior by other employees more difficult.

Higher-level positions, as well as some other white-collar jobs, also tend to be one-of-a-kind positions in the organization (see Labovitz, 1969). Comparing the performance of one employee to that of others in similar jobs (a normative context) is one method commonly used to arrive at appraisal ratings. For unique positions, that context does not exist, and rating performance is more difficult.

Cornelius, Hakel, and Sackett (1979) and Gartland and Tornow (1977) conducted systematic studies of how finely differentiated PA measurement criteria must be to cover all managerial and professional employees. Both studies indicate that rating all these employees on a standard set of criteria is inappropriate. Although they suggest that the PA criteria should vary, nowhere do they state that the overall PA approach (e.g., MBO) must vary.

Individual Differences

The characteristics of individual employees, such as race, gender, and age, can also affect performance ratings. There are widely held stereotypes about the abilities and "proper role" of ethnic minorities, women, and older workers that can affect raters' perceptions of the performance of members of these groups.

Overall, in reviews by Dunnette and Borman (1979) and others, studies were cited that consistently report about the effects of an employee's characteristics on his/her performance ratings. The impact is not as simple as one would predict, based on a traditional theory of prejudice. That is, members of protected classes are not consistently rated lower than their white male counterparts. The results suggest more complexity to the issue when, in some cases, a member of a protected class is rated higher than his/her counterpart.

In some studies, the important issue was whether the rater was similar to the ratee. For example, black and white supervisors gave higher ratings to same-race employees in a study conducted by Crooks (1972). Conversely, Schwab and Heneman (1978) found that older raters gave lower ratings for older employees than did their younger counterparts. Further, there is limited evidence that female workers are generally rated lower than males regardless of the rater (DeCotiis & Petit, 1978).

In brief, the demographic dissimilarities and similarities between rater and ratee introduce important "noise" into the PA system and should be addressed. Significant work has been done to silence this noise by training managers to recognize and reduce some biases in their evaluations (see, e.g., Borman, 1979).

Performance Differences

There has been a long-standing assumption that managers avoid appraising low performers. From the literature, it seems that the major problem with appraising low performers lies not so much in the ratings themselves but in communicating low ratings to the employee. Confronting an employee with bad news is uncomfortable for many people.

In fact, managers may be uncomfortable discussing PAs with low performers, but they do engage in such discussions. Two studies (Feild & Holley, 1977; Fisher, 1979) tested the common assumption that managers avoid giving low performers feedback. Both studies found the opposite. They reported such feedback occurring with less delay than for employees performing above average. However, Fisher (1979) found that if the rater is required to give feedback on the ratings to the low performers, there is a tendency to "inflate" the ratings to make the discussion less uncomfortable.

The suggestion has been made that employees at different overall performance levels be appraised differently. Cummings and Schwab (1973) outlined a compelling rationale and program to structure different PA systems for low, average, and high performers. The factors that distinguish these three approaches include the type of information collected, the frequency of performance reviews, and the role of the employee in the PA process. No test results of this system have appeared yet in the literature.

PA AS FEEDBACK

In some organizations, PA is defined purely in terms of the observation and evaluation process; employees neither receive information about their evaluations nor learn the criteria used for measuring their job performance. In terms of formal policy, however, most organizations recently surveyed reported that employees engage in some form of a feedback process, usually with the immediate supervisor. For example, a 1974 survey conducted by the Bureau of National Affairs showed that PA information was communicated to employees in 91% of 139 organizations (Feild & Holley, 1975). Similar results from another survey showed that appraisal results were discussed with employees in 73–90% of the PA programs (Lacho, Stearns, & Villere, 1979).

Performance feedback usually occurs once or twice a year in formal discussions between the manager and the employee. These discussions are designed to accomplish one or more of the following goals:

1 Establish performance goals, expectations, and standards to maintain or improve performance.
2 Review interim progress to date and solve a performance-related problem.
3 Give the employee information about how he/she is doing overall, often including salary increase information.

It is often assumed that effective performance discussions will lead to performance improvement, increased motivation, enhanced personal development, and greater job satisfaction. Research studies have examined numerous aspects of performance communication between the manager and employee in general (Jablin, 1979) and PA interview sessions specifically (Carroll & Tosi, 1973; Maier, 1958). Performance feedback has been shown to positively influence learning (Hillery & Wexley, 1974; Sassenrath, 1975), motivation (Deci, 1975; Hackman & Oldham, 1976), and, to some degree, job performance (Ilgen, Fisher, & Taylor, 1979).

Jablin (1979) cited the importance of superior-subordinate communication for managing effectively. A key part of clear communication is getting the employee to understand and accept the manager's expectations of what the employee should and should not be doing (Greene, 1975; Pfeffer & Salancik, 1975). PA is one way (certainly to be supplemented by others) to communicate these expectations.

Whereas in principle PA gives the manager a useful medium for sharing these expectations with the employee, we have survey data indicating that the message often gets garbled. Only 24% of the respondents indicated that they knew exactly what they would be evaluated on in their upcoming PA. Even in organizations where formal policy supports performance feedback discussions, manager–employee pairs have reported large discrepancies in the degree to which they even recognized or remembered that PA occurred (Hall & Lawler, 1969).

One Model of Performance Feedback

Ilgen, Fisher, and Taylor (1979) reviewed the literature on the impact feedback has on individual behavior in performance-oriented organizations. These authors' review was organized around a four-stage model of how individuals process and act on performance feedback. The authors defined feedback as "a special case of communication in which some sender (hereafter referred to as a source) conveys a message to a recipient. In the case of feedback, the message comprises information about the recipient" (p. 350). According to this model, a person's perception of feedback depends on three major factors: (*a*) the sender's characteristics, (*b*) the receiver's characteristics, and (*c*) the actual message itself.

The four stages of feedback, according to the model and translated into PA terms, can be described as follows:

Stage 1: Perception of Feedback This stage involves how accurately the employee perceives what the supervisor is saying about his/her performance.

Stage 2: Acceptance of Feedback This stage involves the degree to which the employee believes the PA feedback accurately describes his/her performance.

Stage 3: Desire to Respond This stage involves whether the employee wants to *respond* to the supervisor's feedback.

Stage 4: Intended Response This stage involves the beliefs that the employee develops about the response to the feedback which he/she intends to make.

Again, according to the model, different aspects of the characteristics of the supervisor, the employee, and the feedback message are important at each stage. Further, the degree of success at one stage determines how successful the next stages will be. Obviously, if PA feedback is not accurately perceived by the employee, the employee may be accepting and responding to the wrong message.

Shortcomings of Traditional PA as Performance Feedback

This model of the performance feedback process helps explain why day-to-day feedback is a more effective motivation and performance improvement strategy than annual PA discussions. For example, the model suggests that in the first stage the perceptual set of the receiver and the timing and frequency of the information are important in determining accurate perception. Greller and Herold (1975) surveyed employees about their perceptions of the importance of five feedback sources. The results indicated that employees most valued their own thoughts and feelings as a source of feedback, followed by the task itself, the supervisor (day to day), peers, and finally formal (usually annual) PA. Ongoing feedback from the immediate supervisor was significantly more important to employees than PA that was clearly perceived to be least important as a reliable feedback source.

The typical time interval between performance and PA feedback is usually too long to be perceived by the employee as being significantly related. Also, the infrequency of formal PA feedback (once or twice a year) compared with day-to-day feedback is another communication inadequacy.

If this analysis is extended to the second stage of feedback acceptance, where supervisor credibility (expertise and trust) becomes an important determinant, it is easy to see why many managers in PA discussions experience discomfort and low subordinate acceptance. The nature of PA generally discourages accurate perception of feedback in the first stage. This creates extra pressure on the manager in the second stage to gain acceptance of the feedback and resolve misperceptions productively. The likelihood is that the desired performance improvement expressed by the manager in an annual PA discussion never reaches the response stages (3 and 4) in recognizable form. It is obvious that PA is no substitute for day-to-day feedback as an employee development and performance improvement tool.

Guidelines for Effective PA Interviews

There is some evidence, however, that well-conducted PA feedback sessions do enhance employee development. Wexley (1979) and other reviewers summarize some major findings on performance feedback research that suggest some general guidelines for effective PA interviews:

1 The manager should maintain an attitude of support and constructive effort (Burke & Wilcox, 1969; Maier, 1958; Solem, 1960).
2 Criticizing subordinates leads to employee defensiveness and decreased goal achievement (Meyer, Kay, & French, 1965).
3 Emphasis on mutual problem solving by the manager and employee in problem areas increases feedback effectiveness (Maier, 1958).

4 Subordinate satisfaction with the PA interview is higher when the employee perceives the manager to be inviting his/her participation (Greller, 1975; Nemeroff & Wexley, 1979).
5 Performance improvement following the interview is maximized by establishing and communicating specific goals, objectives, and strategies during the interview (Ilgen, Fisher, & Taylor, 1979; Latham, Mitchell, & Dossett, 1978; Latham & Saari, 1979; Locke, 1968; Nemeroff & Wexley, 1979; Steers & Porter, 1974).

Burke and Wilcox (1969) emphasized the need to identify specific behaviors connected with effective PA interviews so that managers can be trained to conduct more effective interviews. As the PA process becomes more closely identified with feedback as well as with observation and measurement, efforts to increase managerial feedback skills will surely gain momentum.

EMPLOYEE PARTICIPATION

In general, the role of the appraisee in PA has been and continues to be predominantly passive. Although participation in the PA feedback discussion is the most frequent avenue of employee participation, employees can participate in various stages of PA: goal setting, criteria development, data collection, self-rating, problem solving, and feedback. In practice, however, employee participation has been restricted largely to certain forms of PA such as mutual problem solving (Maier, 1958), subordinate participation in an MBO process (Meyer, Kay, & French, 1965), and "rap session" formats (Meyer, 1977).

But what impact does employee involvement have? Wexley, Singh, and Yukl (1973) come closest to measuring the impact of employee involvement on employee performance. They reported greater motivation to improve. Considerably more work supports the impact of involvement on satisfaction: both managers and employees reported being more satisfied (Blake & Mouton, 1961; Fletcher, 1973; Wexley, Singh, & Yukl, 1973). Blake and Mouton (1961) also reported more feeling of "teamness" by manager and employee.

In trying to identify what particular aspects of subordinate involvement account for its impact, Greller (1978) asked respondents to indicate if the various managerial behaviors (e.g., listening to employee's concerns) actually occurred. Unfortunately, few of these standard prescriptions produced responses from employees that the experience was useful or satisfying. What did predict satisfaction was a sense of "ownership," or psychological participation in PA.

Another set of findings involving subordinate participation in PA comes from the goal-setting literature. Latham and Yukl (1975) reviewed five studies that measured the effect of participating in the actual goal-setting process, and they reported inconsistent results. Participative goal setting does seem better (at improving employee performance) but only with certain employee groups and under certain conditions. The results of a recent study by Latham and Saari (1979) allow one to state more positively the importance of participation. The individuals who were involved in the actual setting of goals (as well as measuring success against those targets) and were given support by the experimenter, set higher goals (than those who were not involved) and actually performed at higher levels. Although this study took place in a laboratory with college students as subjects, it should be taken seriously because of its rigorous look at the actual interpersonal processes employee involvement is likely to include.

Latham and Saari (1979) cite one important barrier to providing a supportive, participative appraisal experience: it takes considerable time. It involves a process (requiring the presence of both manager and employee) that can easily get sidetracked. This recognition of Latham and Saari is rare in the literature. Seldom are such constraints faced by managers considered in PA research designs.

Involving employees in appraisal is a delicate matter. Rosen (1967), for example, found that those supervisory skills most important to getting employee participation were found least likely to be present in the managerial population. In other words, involving employees does not come naturally to managers.

Subordinate participation in the appraisal process has been extended to actually evaluating his/her manager. The use of subordinate feedback is increasing in the corporate community, as evidenced by the review of Morrison, McCall, and DeVries (1978) of 24 instruments used in organizations for subordinates' evaluations of their managers. Morrison, McCall, and DeVries note specifically that the effectiveness of this survey feedback approach rests on using the information for development purposes only (no repercussions for the manager) and preserving anonymity for the subordinate (e.g., by having a third party compile and process the ratings). These conditions make subordinate-to-manager feedback awkward to fit into the existing PA scenario. But perhaps there are ways that subordinate ratings could be used in appraisal without impeding the feedback process. Research has been done on using student ratings of faculty for administrative purposes (Bernardin, Beatty, & Jensen, 1980). Employee attitude surveys in some corporations also use subordinate evaluations of their managers to make administrative decisions. Considerably more experimentation with subordinate appraisal of managers must be completed before it can be recommended for use in PA.

Involving the employee in the appraisal process is an investment with both costs and returns. The costs include sharing control of the PA process, a change some managers are not likely to take kindly. There is also the risk of introducing data (in the form of self-ratings) that present a different picture of how the employee is doing (a problem if consistency or consensus is a priority). Another cost is the required time (sometimes of an unknown amount) to involve the employee. The return is likely to be a psychological one: both manager and employee will probably be more satisfied with the entire process and perhaps even create more open communication. However, the impact of the process on actual employee performance is, at this point, unclear.

IN CONCLUSION

This chapter focused on the individuals most directly involved in the PA process, recognizing that appraisal is a personal event. The role of appraiser is typically filled by the manager, often imperfectly. Alternative raters were examined, including the employee's subordinates, peers, and the employee himself/herself. None of these alternative raters is likely to generate more accurate ratings than the manager. Unfortunately, tests of some raters—such as subordinates—are incomplete, and we must await a better-defined answer. More positively, self-ratings may be useful to include, not necessarily because of their superior psychometric properties but because employee participation can improve the overall quality of the PA process. In general, we recommend that multiple rating sources be included, if only informally, to act as a check on the incomplete picture generated by any one rater. Formal training for raters is also strongly recommended.

Characteristics of the employee being appraised also have an impact on PA. The employee's race, sex, level of performance, and position in the organization can all influence the appraisal process. PA system designers should recognize these effects and create systems responsive to different employee needs. Finally, the supervisor conducting a formal PA interview, although apparently defying many of the essential criteria for effective feedback, appears to be a continuing reality. As such, the literature provides some limited guidance in maximizing the benefits of formal PA feedback.

THE BOTTOM LINE

The manager as rater The search for a rater to replace the manager has not provided any obviously superior alternatives. The manager is likely to continue being the source for rating employees. That possibility, combined with the documented vagaries of supervisory ratings, places substantial pressure on increasing managers' skill and interest in doing PA.

Multiple raters As organizations take on more complex structures, the issue of multiple raters becomes more vexing. In particular, in matrix or project-oriented structures, evaluation data should be gleaned from several raters. These data could well be integrated by the supervisor into an overall evaluation. In other words, managers should be asked to incorporate ratings of others in situations where the employee has several dotted-line relationships. Only by thoroughly testing multiple rater PA systems in their organizational settings will we learn their relevance for broader use.

PA feedback—an unnatural process As shown in this chapter, the typical PA procedure violates several major prerequisites of effective feedback. Clearly, PA should not be used as the only source of feedback. What PA should do is to build on the more regular, informal ways managers receive and give feedback.

5

Performance Appraisal in Perspective

Why is it that we can point to so many examples of where performance appraisals go wrong and can't come up with any examples of things going right? Don't some appraisal approaches work well? (a human resource manager)

Most organizations are dissatisfied with their performance appraisal (PA) process, particularly for administrative managerial positions. They have concerns about its objectivity, its relevance and its validity. In many cases the complaint is that the appraisal system simply does not work! (Schneier & Beatty, 1979, p. 65)

These two bleak assessments of the state of the PA art reflect a range of symptoms of PA systems gone awry. They include the following:

1 Formal PA programs "vanishing" as one questions managers and then their subordinates about what actually happens (Porter, Lawler, & Hackman, 1975).
2 An almost constant reassessment by organizations of their appraisal systems. Most PA systems have remarkably short lives (Lazer & Wikstrom, 1977).
3 PA systems that create global ratings for use in pay decisions often create little differentiation among employees (often 80% or more are rated as "outstanding") (Bell, 1979; Patten, 1977).
4 Employee attitude surveys frequently show that the PA system is a major source of dissatisfaction. For example, only 27% of managerial and professional employees in an organization surveyed by the authors reported being satisfied with the way their appraisal was done.

These facts lead one to ask some tough questions about PA systems: Are there PA systems out there that work? What do we mean when we say "work"? How do we evaluate PA systems?

The present chapter addresses the issue of effectiveness of PA systems through the following sections: "Effectiveness Criteria" (How do we know if PA is working?), "Evaluating PA Systems" (What does the literature say about the effectiveness of each system?), and "Unresolved Issues" (Why does the literature provide so little help in selecting systems? What can I do in the interim?).

EFFECTIVENESS CRITERIA

One reality of the PA literature is the narrow-minded approach taken toward the issue of defining PA effectiveness. A useful analogy to understand this narrowness is business computers, another organizational tool developed in the past two decades. Translating PA evaluation efforts into their counterparts for computers would have resulted in a focus on internal programming issues, creating more sophisticated hardware but all along ignoring software issues as well as the actual uses organizations wanted to make of the computers. In fact, the explosion of computer use for business is occurring largely because the software issues are being addressed and because of a sensitive response to specific concerns of management (such as inventory profiling).

The PA technicians have only recently shown sensitivity to the fact that PA is a tool for management and that the tool will be used if, and only if, it proves effective (more specifically, cost effective) in meeting certain needs. Historically, PA researchers have evaluated PA approaches by testing whether they increase convergent and discriminant validities simultaneously. Meanwhile, the management community is asking whether PA ratings can be relied on to make judgments about employees and whether the system can be used efficiently. Recent approaches in the literature (Beer & Ruh, 1976; Patten, 1977; Schneier & Beatty, 1979) are beginning to recognize that PA is an organizational tool and, as such, should be evaluated with the users' needs in mind.

Conversations we had with managers about alternative PA systems inevitably led to questions about both the costs and relative effectiveness of any PA system. This ratio of cost to potential outcomes provides a useful model for evaluating existing PA systems. The following list of key cost items and potential outcomes was generated from surveys of existing PA practices (see Chapter 2) and the authors' experience in evaluating PA systems.

Major PA costs are the following:

1 System development (costs are primarily staff time, perhaps outside consultants).

- **a** Assess goals and current status.
- **b** Create policies.
- **c** Generate forms.
- **d** Design training programs.
- **e** Change related human resource programs as needed.

2 System introduction (staff time).

- **a** Conduct training for managers.
- **b** Revise the system (get the bugs out).
- **c** Handle possible employee resistance (new, additional forms).

3 System maintenance (staff time).

- **a** Amount of managerial and subordinate time required to do the appraisal.
- **b** Number of "problem cases" requiring help of personnel function.

Major PA outcomes are the following:

1 Meet goals for PA as a human resource system (Chapter 2 cites the following five commonly cited goals organizations have for PA).

- **a** Input to administrative decisions (salary increases, promotions, etc.).
  - 1 Need to rank employees comparatively on standardized, global dimensions of current performance and potential performance in higher positions.
- **b** Develop employees.
  - 1 Need to look specifically at both how employees perform and their overall contribution to organizationally relevant goals.
  - 2 Requires a 12-month process (see Chapter 1) of setting expectations, monitoring performance, reviewing performance with the employee, and making action plans for employee improvement.
- **c** Identify training needs.
  - 1 Need an analysis of the specific behaviors required by an employee to perform his/her job.
  - 2 Requires an organizational audit of performance trends, focusing on skill deficit areas.
- **d** Help do human resource planning (Answer such questions as "Are there enough high-performing first-line managers to satisfy our future need for general managers?" or "Are our 'protected class' managers performing well?").
  - 1 Need easy access to overall evaluations of employees throughout the organization.

- **e** Help in legal documentation (Note: many selection procedures in organizations are defended on their ability to predict subsequent PA ratings).
  1 Need evidence that PA is job relevant.
  2 Show emphasis on behavior- or outcome-related criteria.
  3 Should have evidence of an informed employee.
  4 Need procedures and data demonstrating a systematic and objective administration of the PA process.

2 Organizational acceptance.
- **a** Managerial receptivity.
  1 Managers should be willing to implement the PA system thoroughly.
  2 Managers should find PA of some value and worth the investment.
- **b** Employee (recipient) receptivity.
  1 Employees should report receiving PA.
  2 Employees should find receiving PA valuable, with feedback seen as accurate.
- **c** Top-management support.
  1 Executives should be able to articulate the role PA plays in managing employees: why PA is done, how PA should be done, and how PA relates to other human resource programs.
  2 Executives should be able to cite information on actual uses of the PA system.

We are suggesting that some subset of the foregoing issues should enter the mind of a human resource professional any time a PA system revision is considered. Do not infer that a PA system must meet all these outcomes. Only a subset can be met. One of the unfortunate trends in PA has been that its advocates have promised too much.

Obviously missing from the list just provided are weightings of the various criteria. These weightings must be, and typically are, applied to each organization. For example, management may decide, on the outcome side, that legal documentation is the primary reason for upgrading PA, since the organization recently lost a class-action discrimination suit. The PA system to be designed would therefore focus on creating legal viability rather than employee development or another possible goal.

The summary of the cost-effectiveness model in Exhibit 12 also contains information about who incurs the costs and who receives the benefits of PA. The organization is divided into line and staff functions, with human resource professionals of primary interest in the staff function. Assigning the

Exhibit 12 Summary of Cost-Effectiveness Model of PA System

Costs (to whom)	*Outcomes* (for whom)
Develop system (staff)	Input to administrative decisions (staff and line)
Introduce system (staff and line)	Develop employees (line)
Maintain system (line)	Identify training needs (staff)
	Help human resource planning (staff)
	Legal documentation (staff)
	Organizational acceptance and credibility (line and staff)

costs and benefits to these two groups can be useful for predicting receptivity to a new PA system. For example, if PA requires a great deal of time and energy from the manager and is focused on meeting the legal documentation outcome, a classic conflict situation exists: the major costs are borne by line employees, and the major benefits are received by staff employees. As we see later, one PA system (BARS) may be in exactly that situation, and the reception of this system in the managerial community is at best ambivalent.

In practice, organizations appear to be uniquely responsive to some of the criteria (on both the cost and outcome sides) and unresponsive to others. Although the literature does not address this issue, we have found that executives in organizations are particularly sensitive to implementation costs. The executives are concerned about how many additional forms the manager will need to fill out, how many meetings with the employee will be required and when during the year, and so on. On the outcome side, executives seem to feel that the acceptance and credibility of the PA system in the organization is very important. Whereas the other outcomes may be accepted as real by top management, evidence regarding effectiveness is often so obscure that it does not enter the decision-making process.

In short, the model presented here can be used to evaluate any organization's existing PA system or another PA system being considered for use. The model is unique in that it focuses on both costs and returns to the organization. Applying it to any organization requires assigning a weight to each criterion.

EVALUATING PA SYSTEMS

This set of criteria can provide a revealing profile for any PA system mentioned in the literature. First, however, we need to define a PA system.

The literature is replete with examples of PA approaches that leave many questions unanswered. The literature on subordinate participation in PA (e.g., Maier, 1958; Wexley, Singh, & Yukl, 1973) is a good example of a theme that does not constitute a PA system. The participation literature does not provide paradigms for answering basic questions such as what purposes can PA serve and how can performance be measured, much less how should PA relate to other personnel programs. The subordinate participation theme is often embedded in PA systems (such as MBO).

A PA system should give the user some guidance, if not specific answers to each of the five basic questions asked by a good journalist: Who? What? When? Where? Why? Exhibit 13 translates each of these five questions into an issue specific to PA. These five issues, suggested by Lazer and Wikstrom (1977) and Haynes (1978), represent dimensions of PA on which any designer of an organization-specific PA program must take a position.

Exhibit 13 Necessary Components of Any PA System

Generic Question	PA Specific Issue
Who?	Appropriate employee populations (e.g., managerial, professional, nonexempt)
What?	Cycle of events Does prescribe sequence of Set expectations → monitor performance → evaluation and document performance → feedback to employee? Are performance expectations job relevant? Is process for feedback explicitly defined? Are procedures available to train participants?
When?	Relate PA events chronologically to other management programs
Where?	Functional relations to other management programs (e.g., strategic planning, compensation)
Why?	Primary purposes served (e.g., employee development or salary administration)

Exhibit 13 is valuable not only for identifying generic PA systems but also for human resource managers to evaluate the completeness of a PA program. By articulating issues such as the need to specify PA feedback processes, a human resource manager can pinpoint areas of potential confusion within the PA system. Only recently has the literature suggested critical components in designing a PA system (see, e.g., Beer & Ruh, 1976; Haynes, 1978).

Several criteria were used in selecting PA systems to evaluate:

1 The system should take a stand on the majority of the who, what, when, where, and why questions.
2 Some empirical evidence regarding the system's effectiveness should be available.
3 At least one actual organizational use of the system should be reported in the literature.

In the process we rejected such approaches as subordinate participation (Maier, 1958), the performance contingent approach (Maintenance Action Program, Developmental Action Program, and Remedial Action Program; see Cummings & Schwab, 1973), and the trait-rating scale approach (Lopez, 1968). The classic graphic-rating approach was excluded because the behavior-based PA system we do review represents to us the "best can" argument one can make for the graphic-rating approach. Also, when the trait-rating approach is referred to in the literature, it is often as a "control condition" to show the superiority of a newly developed alternative approach.

The appalling result was that only three PA systems were left to review. These three systems selected are compared along the five dimensions in Exhibit 14. The PA systems are labeled "behavior based," "effectiveness based," and "hybrid." Schneier and Beatty (1979) provided the basis for distinguishing among the three systems.

Behavior-based PA

This approach has taken several forms, with BARS and BES being the two most refined systems. The general approach is to create PA performance dimensions that rely on job-relevant behaviors (Smith & Kendall, 1963). Specific procedures for identifying the behavioral criteria were explained in Chapter 3.

Taylor (1976) described the development and actual use of a BARS appraisal system for managers in the insurance industry. Gartland and Tornow (1977) also defined the parameters of a behaviorally based appraisal program developed as part of a larger attempt to integrate human resource programs at Control Data Corporation. Beatty, Schneier, and Beatty (1977) reported efforts by organizations to design BARS systems.

The behavior-based approach is defined in more specific terms in Exhibit 14. Take special note that BARS is probably appropriate for no higher positions than first-level managers and that it focuses on meeting the needs of administrative decisions (such as pay), whereas feedback to the subordinate is less critical.

Exhibit 14 Three PA Systems: Descriptive Profiles

Critical System Dimension	Behavior Based (e.g., BARS)	Effectiveness Based (e.g., MBO)	Hybrid
Who?			
Employee population	First-line management and below	From top-level management to nonexempt	Middle management to professional
Why?			
Principal purposes	Administrative decisions Legal documentation	Develop employee	Develop employee Administrative decisions
What?			
Critical events specified	Final year-end evaluation	Minimum of two meetings Ongoing monitoring	Same as MBO
Procedure for measuring job relevance	General position cluster	Highly individualized	Combines the two
Feedback process defined	Afterthought	Well defined	Well defined; two types of feedback
Training of participants	Yes—focus on rating process	Yes—focus on goal setting	Yes—focus on both goal setting and feedback
When?			
Chronologically placed	Specified—salary review time	Yes—coincide with business planning	Same as MBO
Where?			
Specify role	Yes—center of personnel programs	Yes—in context of business planning	Yes—personnel programs

The effectiveness of behavior-based PA systems is profiled in Exhibit 15. This figure contains judgments by the authors regarding both the costs and likely outcomes for each of the three PA systems. Judgments that have received direct support in the PA literature appear in bold. It is immediately apparent that few effectiveness issues have been addressed in the literature.

Exhibit 15 Cost-Effectiveness of Three Principal PA Systems in the Literature[a]

	Behavior Based (e.g., BARS)	Effectiveness Based (e.g., MBO)	Hybrid
Costs			
Develop the system (e.g., create the form)	**High**	Low	High
Introduce the system (e.g., train managers)	Moderate	High	High
Maintain the system (e.g., time of managers required; amount of paperwork)	Low	**High**	High
Outcomes			
Chance of fulfilling purposes			
Valid input to administrative decisions (e.g., pay)	**Moderate**	Low	Moderate
Develop employee (e.g., improve performance)	Low	**Moderate**	Moderate
Identify training needs of employees	Moderate	Low	Moderate
Help human resource planning	Low	Low	Moderate
Give legal documentation	**High**	Moderate	High
Organizational acceptance	**Low**	**Moderate**	Low

[a] Judgments shown in boldface type are those for which the literature provides direct evidence for the judgment.

The high cost of developing BARS (Borman, 1978) comes mainly from the time needed for large samples of managers to make repeated judgments about desired and undesired behaviors. The moderate rating for "Valid input to administrative decisions" is based on both the Gartland and Tornow (1977) description of the appropriateness of such PA data for other systems and on reviews of the reliability and validity of BARS-generated ratings (Dunnette & Borman, 1979; Schwab, Heneman, & DeCotiis, 1975; Vance, Kuhnert, & Farr, 1978).

The low rating for organizational acceptance reflects the few actual instances of BARS in use by organizations (see, e.g., Lazer & Wikstrom,

1977). BARS must be one of the most researched and least-used management tools in modern management history. DeCotiis (1977) studied the receptivity of managers to BARS compared with a trait-rating system and an instrument designed by the managers themselves (Numerically Anchored Rating Scales). DeCotiis found that BARS was least valued for such uses as those cited here:

1 Helping counsel the employee about how to improve his/her performance.
2 Ease of understanding of the PA system itself.
3 Identifying needs of the employee for training in specific skill areas.

To summarize, the behavior-based PA system appears to entail high development costs but is relatively inexpensive to implement (in terms of time required). The system's effectiveness is primarily limited to providing legal documentation and valid input for other administrative decisions. Its acceptance by those who are asked to use it is not likely to be terribly positive.

Effectiveness-based PA

A major focus of recent PA literature has been on evaluating employees in terms of their effectiveness in achieving important outcomes. This approach emphasizes more than simply a unique measurement strategy. It entails establishing desired outcomes through a discussion between a manager and an employee, translating those outcomes into agreed-on measures, and periodically monitoring actual performance against the expectations. This approach has found its way into the literature under the guise of MBO and goal setting.

The dimensions critical to effectiveness-based PA (see Exhibit 14) reveal an emphasis on creating useful feedback to the employee. MBO, for example, fits directly into the larger business-planning programs used by management. The cost-effectiveness picture (see Exhibit 15) reveals substantial costs for introducing and implementing the system.

On the effectiveness end of the equation, a review by Latham and Yukl (1975) of the goal-setting and MBO literature revealed reasonably consistent evidence of some improvement in employee performance. In a thorough evaluation of an MBO program, Ivancevich (1972, 1974) suggested, however, that MBO by itself has little impact. Only when MBO is given top-management support are any effects on performance likely to be noted. The moderate rating for organizational acceptance comes partly from Lazer and Wikstrom's (1977) survey in which 54 of the 72 respondents from organizations using MBO reported that it is "effective."

In short, effectiveness-based systems, although entailing low development costs, are expensive to introduce and maintain. The outcomes that MBO and related programs are likely to achieve are limited to developing the employee, with user acceptance also likely to be reasonably good. MBO gives little direct help in meeting other often-cited goals for PA.

Hybrid PA

The hybrid approach is the current vogue in PA. Porter, Lawler, and Hackman (1975) stated that a hybrid approach is useful because a full (and accurate) picture of job performance requires measuring both behaviors and outcomes. This combination has been advocated by several MBO proponents (Bishop, 1974; Brady, 1973; Levinson, 1976) and BARS advocates (Schneier & Beatty, 1979).

The development of a hybrid PA system at Corning Glass Works has been described in some detail (Beer & Ruh, 1976; Beer et al., 1978). Called the "Performance Management System" (PMS), it consists of three parts:

1 Management by objectives—a traditional MBO planning, documenting, and reviewing sequence.
2 Performance development review—rating on behavioral dimensions on a standardized performance profile.
3 Performance results evaluation—an overall rating of the employee's performance used for administrative decisions.

The Beer et al. (1978) study described the reaction of managers to this PA system at Corning. The data suggest that the managers using PMS found this particular PA system reasonably useful, although the authors noted that user acceptance could have been greater had the organization invested more in its implementation.

Profiles of the hybrid approach (see Exhibits 14 and 15) can be described as "complete" or "intensive." Hybrid PA has been designed to cover the weaknesses or limits of both the behavior-based and effectiveness-based appraisal systems. Whereas BARS appears to be particularly responsive to administrative uses and MBO seems most appropriate for developing employees, the hybrid approach attempts to achieve both.

The costs and outcomes picture indicates that a hybrid approach involves high costs to design, introduce, and implement. In return, the organization gets a system that (although not well substantiated in the literature) is likely to meet several goals often set for PA systems. The low rating for organizational acceptance reflects the judgment we have that managers may perceive they are being asked to give too much to this process.

Beer et al. (1978) and others (Levinson, 1976; Porter, Lawler, & Hackman, 1975; Shakman & Roberts, 1977) have proposed hybrid PA systems; however, the evidence supporting the additional investment required is, at this point, conceptual rather than empirical. It is difficult to argue with the notion that PA should give a complete picture of performance and that such a picture requires assessing both what an individual accomplishes and how he/she reaches those ends. What is desperately needed is solid empirical evidence to back these assumptions.

Summary of PA Effectiveness

The review we have presented of three principal PA systems covered in the literature reveals that all involve substantial costs (in managerial and staff time) in the development, introduction, and maintenance stages. In return for that investment, one is likely to achieve at best moderate results on only one or two of the five uses often cited for PA. The one PA system that does promise more widespread use is at this point unproved.

Another aspect of PA systems not included in the previous review is their tolerance of abuse. Court cases involving claims of discrimination (Cascio & Bernardin, in press) may be one result of misuse of PA systems. PA can be used by managers to act out their prejudices, whether they are directed at minorities, women, or older individuals. Another form of abuse is the lack of response in managers' ratings to changes in an employee's performance over time (witness the incredible predictability of ratings from one year to the next) or to the natural differences in the level of performance for employees.

Effectiveness-based systems are most open to abuse because they rely almost totally on a conscientious and objective treatment of the employees by the manager. In contrast, behavior-based systems such as BARS are designed to be "foolproof." That is, the manager is given the relevant dimensions on which the employee is to be rated and shown concrete behaviors which indicate whether the employee did well on that dimension. Effectiveness-based systems derive their strength from the flexibility they give the manager—both in deciding what the employee should be doing and what constitutes success. This flexibility opens up the system to abuse by managers.

Overall, organizations are being asked to invest heavily in an imperfect management tool. Some imperfections are common to all PA systems; others center on matching a PA system to a set of employees, uses, and so forth. Both types of imperfections are important in designing and using PA.

UNRESOLVED ISSUES

What are Reasonable Goals for PA?

PA is expected to serve many needs of organizations and individuals. As Schneier and Beatty (1979) stated, PA cannot be all things to all people. The PA systems documented most thoroughly (BARS and MBO) suggest that one must choose. In this case the choice seems to be between a system that directly helps the employee versus one which provides information for making various personnel decisions. Although the hybrid approach seeks to meet a much broader range of needs, its success has yet to be proved. In the interim one must ask if PA systems fail because too many goals (some of which may be conflicting) are set for them.

There Is Little Incentive to Invest in PA

A repeated theme in the literature (e.g., Ivancevich, 1974; McCall & DeVries, 1977) is the lack of sufficient investment by management in PA systems. PA is a complex process requiring trained managers willing to give the process considerable time. One suspects the reason many PA systems fail is that managers were never willing to apply more than a token amount of energy to the task. On the other hand, management has, as a rule, been given little reason (either from their own past experience or from the "experts") to invest heavily in PA.

The Search for Simple Programs Creates Inflexibility

As Schneier and Beatty (1979) pointed out, jobs change regularly, particularly for managerial and professional employees. PA criteria, on the other hand, stay constant and revising them seems almost an unnatural act. Keeley (1978) has tackled this issue by generating a "judgment based" PA process designed specifically for jobs with high task uncertainty. This system uses multiple raters, accepts the subjectivity of evaluations, and recognizes that jobs can change in focus more frequently than once a year. Whether such options could ever be widely accepted for use as PA remains to be seen.

PA Programs are Boxed in by Assumed Constraints

The current PA systems cited in the literature share many features, resulting in a sense that "nothing new is happening." One example of a common feature is the use of the immediate manager as the appraiser. The literature is replete with evidence that the manager's perspective is limited. It is limited by his/her biases, incomplete information regarding the employee's total performance, and the unique role the manager plays vis-à-vis the employee (dispenser of rewards, protector, etc.). One suspects that little progress will be made if these limiting assumptions are not directly challenged.

Implementation of PA Systems Is Often Spotty

Even with "innovative" PA programs, the actual use of such programs can be and often is less than desired. What so few PA systems in the literature have recognized is the very real stake the employee has in receiving a fair, thorough PA. Dwyer and Dimitroff (1976) reported an innovative "Bottom Up/Top Down" PA approach that gives the employee receiving the appraisal a legitimate role as evaluator of the PA process. Such forms of monitoring PA that are integral to the process itself are welcome additions to the literature.

Until such unresolved issues as those just cited are actively addressed in the PA literature, PA report cards are likely to continue to report marginal, if not failing, grades.

IN CONCLUSION

This chapter focused on the question, "What PA systems 'work'?" To answer this question, we applied several criteria to three PA systems to reflect both likely costs to the organization and potential outcomes. Only three PA systems have been described in enough detail to warrant review: behavior based, effectiveness based, and a hybrid (both behavior and effectiveness measures included). Comparing behavior-based with effectiveness-based PA systems is most informative, since the two complement each other: one is strong where the other is weak. Although the hybrid approach promises to be the best of both possible worlds, solid empirical evidence to support this claim is scanty. We conclude by speculating about why the state of the PA art is so problematic. Several overriding limits of all PA approaches are cited, including spotty, half-hearted implementation by organizations.

THE BOTTOM LINE

No PA system has been shown "to work" If the overriding question of this chapter is "What works?" then the answer is "We don't know." We do know what does not work. Traditional trait-oriented graphic-rating scales may be easy to implement, but what they give you is not likely to stand up to any tests—particularly those a court of law is likely to apply.

In principle, the hybrid system appears to cover best all the bases. It should be useful both in helping make administrative decisions and for giving the employee useful feedback. Five years from now we should be in a better position to judge the impact of hybrid systems. A hybrid system should be treated as a second- or third-generation PA system. It is unlikely to work in an organization with no prior PA program or in an organization recently "burned" by PA (i.e., asked to invest much in PA with little return).

But what does it mean "to work"? Some of the most difficult work in reassessing existing or creating new PA systems is in identifying a finite set of goals for the system. Until you do so, making changes in the mechanics of the system can be a random act. Defining and limiting the goals of PA are so difficult because PA involves multiple constituencies both in and outside the organization.

Commonalities among PA systems are impressive Whereas the focus of the chapter was on comparing and contrasting several PA systems, one is also struck by the systems' commonalities, particularly what is required for any PA system to work. Those are as follows:

1 Informed participants: all individuals—top management, managers in general, and employees—need to know why and how they are to do PA.
2 PA looks to the future and past: PA is not just a review of the past 12 months; all three PA systems also included a statement of expectations—a look at the upcoming 12 months. Any PA system must clearly define for the employee what is expected.

Successful PA is an ephemeral experience Even in organizations in which PA is being done regularly and competently by managers there still seems to be a top management that remains unconcerned about the merit of its procedure. The reason may reside in the list of outcomes typically assigned to PA (see Exhibit 15). PA is asked to serve other human resource programs. Even if PA does serve these other programs successfully, it is a step away from the more primary goal of a more efficient and humane use of the human resources in the organization. Measuring this latter goal requires translating human resources into financial terms. Employees can be viewed as significant assets in organizations, assets that should be capitalized on. Dahl (1979) and others are developing human resource accounting models that will give organizations more tangible goals for their human resource programs. The value of translating human resource programs into financial impact can be seen in the Mirvis and Lawler (1977) study of attitude surveys. Applying such accounting procedures is a much-needed and promising redefinition of the goals of such human resource programs as PA.

6

Implementing Performance Appraisal in Organizations

Many times . . . I have come to realize that a fervent speech, or a painstakingly written document, may be worth no more than the good will and patient cooperation of those who say they subscribe to it. The multiplication of documents, resolutions, exhortations, and declamatory documents seems to be the major growth business of the age. I fear that we too often lay more stress on words than on the stark necessity of deeds to back them up. . . .*

Item: After examining the results of a general employee attitude survey, corporate staff of the R Corporation were persuaded to establish a formal corporate-wide PA policy and procedure. A two-page MBO-type form, complete with a five-step procedure and appropriate column headings printed at the top of the first page, was sent to all managerial personnel on the corporate mailing list. Accompanying the form was a corporate memorandum from top management that read:

It is the policy of the R Corporation to ensure that all employees are evaluated on at least an annual basis in a timely and equitable manner. As of this date, all managerial personnel will use the enclosed Form R—80759, entitled "Performance Appraisal Record," to accomplish this purpose. . . . We are looking forward to the success of this program.

Three years later, after examining the "less than encouraging" results of the most recent general employee attitude survey, corporate staff were persuaded to "reestablish" the formal, corporate-wide PA policy.

Getting a PA system from paper to practice is a difficult process. Although the literature concentrates on the critical aspects of system design, practitioners are often left wondering how even a well-designed PA program

*Excerpt from *At Ease: Stories I Tell My Friends* by Dwight D. Eisenhower, Copyright © 1967 by Dwight D. Eisenhower. Reprinted by permission of Doubleday & Company, Inc.

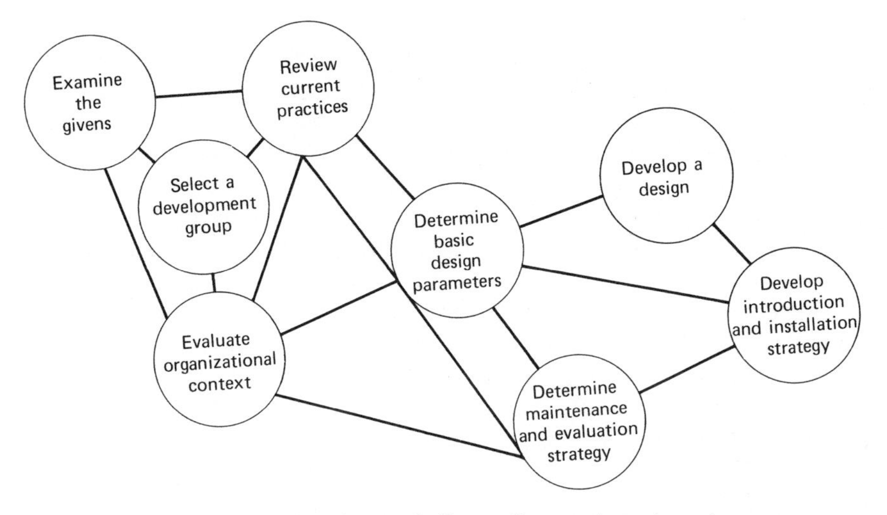

Figure 4 PA implementation: Some stepping stones.

can become an operational reality in their organizations. Unfortunately, many PA systems, usually designed by a few personnel staff members, are briefly introduced into organizations in a manner like that used in Corporation R—primarily as a new form, with a brief cover memo from the personnel department. As Eisenhower noted, it is then assumed that this distribution procedure is the same as practice. The fallacy of this assumption is often discovered much later, through the grisly results of attitude surveys or the limited defenses mustered in the courtroom.

This chapter takes the perspective that *how* a PA system is put into an organization is as critical as *what* the technology of that PA system is. It further assumes that, just as PA on the individual level is a process and not merely a series of isolated events, putting a PA system into place is also not an event; it is a process of organizational intervention.

The PA literature has focused largely on the development of increasingly sophisticated measurement and feedback technologies. In fact, most PA system types are named for the measurement strategy employed, as if the process of selecting the "right" PA system for any given organization was akin to finding the right wrench size in a Sears catalog.

The literature on implementing PA, however, is limited. That which does exist is highly prescriptive and based on either other literatures (such as organizational development) or personal experiences, anecdotally described in informal, "first-person" articles. Thus, in addressing implementation, we are forced to move a step or two away from the formal PA literature. Such a move is necessary because PA is not just an issue of sophisticated measurement or feedback technology; it is an organizational system that must be considered in light of the realities of organizational life.

In fact, implementation of a PA system is a continuing process involving complex issues of design, installation, and maintenance. Some of the key issues involved are shown in Figure 4. These issues are envisioned as operational "stepping stones," much like the primitive paths one uses to navigate a stream. Just as two individuals neither cross a stream in the same manner nor even start or finish in the same place, no two organizations or work units will implement PA systems in exactly the same way. These stepping stones, however, do provide a flexible framework from which we can present generic organizational considerations critical to the success of any PA system. This chapter examines these stepping stones as aspects of design, installation, and maintenance.

PA DESIGN: SOME STEPPING STONES

The implementation of a PA system begins on the first occasion design is considered.

Examine the Givens

Most organizations today are not in the position of having to design a formal PA system "from scratch" for the first time. Numerous surveys have documented the prevalence of formal policies and procedures (see Chapter 2). These same surveys have also shown spotty use of such policies and procedures and even less satisfaction with their effectiveness in practice (Porter, Lawler, & Hackman, 1975).

The more pivotal question appears to be "How often should a PA system be revised?" In a study of 18 major corporations, Teel (1980) found that the trend is toward frequent revision (every one to five years) and gradually evolving change (as opposed to a major overhaul). Teel concluded that:

> Chances are that this iterative process will be never-ending, because changes in jobs and in the composition of the work force will, over time, necessitate further changes in appraisal systems. Even those systems that are working well today will undoubtedly have to be changed sometime in the future. (Teel, 1980, p. 301)

Thus, before organizations launch major design or redesign efforts directed at improving PA systems, it is critical to examine givens such as those named next:

1 What problems or issues have created the need for design or redesign?
2 What existing organizational commitment is there for a design/redesign effort?
3 What can realistically be done during a specified time period?
4 What resources exist to carry out the work?
5 How important is it to design or revise the formal PA system?

Select a Development Group

Most PA systems are designed by the company's corporate-level personnel department (about 73–75%, according to Lazer & Wikstrom, 1977); divisional personnel staff sometimes develop systems (7–15%), as do internal and external consultants (3–4% and 3–8%, respectively).

There are three general groups of people who could participate in the design stage: outside consultants, internal human resource specialists, and line managers or other employees. There are advantages and disadvantages to having any one of these groups design a PA system.

Outside consultants who specialize in PA systems are most likely to have the expertise and technical knowledge to design a psychometrically sound PA program. Although they may recognize the need to integrate PA with other organizational systems, they will not be as familiar with the policies or actual practices that characterize these other systems. Thus, the ability of outside consultants to design a PA program to fit a particular organization may be limited. Also, because these consultants' services can be very expensive, their involvement in the process may be limited to short periods of time or may be too costly.

Internal human resource specialists may not have the in-depth knowledge of current PA technology, but they do have a better working knowledge of the personnel systems and (perhaps) other business systems being used by the organization than outside consultants. However, PA is often viewed by managers as a personnel gimmick (see, e.g., Nystrom, 1977), and the personnel staff may be unable to muster the needed support and clout to ensure use of the PA system (see, e.g., Kanter, 1979). But although external consultants come and go, the personnel staff or internal consultants continue to oversee the PA program long after its design and may develop a thorough understanding of, and commitment to, the PA program that continues into the later stages of implementation.

Line managers and other employees are both the primary users of PA and those most familiar with day-to-day operations and the nature of the work being evaluated. Whereas these employees are typically not familiar with the technical aspects of PA systems, they are in a unique position to provide realistic and accurate information about performance criteria and workable appraisal methods. The participation of these employees in the design stage can lead to a practical PA program that managers and other employees will find believable.

One strategy used by some organizations in designing a PA program is to involve all three of these groups. For example, an external consultant may work with one or more task forces, comprised of personnel department staff as well as experienced managers (and perhaps professional employees), to design a PA program. Each group of participants is able to contribute unique information in the design process. The external consultant may take a limited role in identifying alternatives and the general advantages and disadvantages of each, and the staff and line employees use their own perspectives in evaluating alternatives and arriving at an appropriate PA program.

The design team should be carefully selected so that members have not only the knowledge and perspectives needed to develop a PA program but also credibility within the organization and the access to top management needed to win acceptance of the program. The team should represent major segments of the organization (such as manufacturing, marketing, etc.) yet be kept to a reasonable size (about 6 to 10 members). Members must also be prepared to devote the required time to the design effort (DeVries, 1979).

Review PA and Related Practices

Before design begins, it is helpful to identify and evaluate the current situation with regard to PA. This can include an examination of the oganization's PA policies and practices (both historically and currently), other human resource programs (salary, promotion, career development, etc.), other feedback systems, legal status, management philosophy, organizational "climate," and the like (see, e.g., McCall, 1978).

A survey of employees (using questionnaires and interviews) is sometimes used to assess the strengths and weaknesses of the existing PA program and to help identify what employees want from PA. Also, organizations sometimes gather information about PA systems used successfully in other companies, although a PA program designed for one organization may have to be modified to work in another.

Evaluate the Organizational Context

Several authors have recently begun to address the context into which a PA system must be integrated to survive (Kane & Lawler, 1979; McCall & DeVries, 1977; Wexley, 1979). Contextual factors interface with or are outside the structure of the PA system itself and yet are part of the larger organizational system in which a PA system must exist. Failure to recognize and address these factors from the design stage can severely limit the success of any PA program. Consider the following six contextual factors.

Consistency with management philosophy and practice Most PA programs are established in the middle of highly structured hierarchical organizations. In such organizations, responsibility for strategic issues is clearly the prerogative of higher-level management, and in the manager–employee pair responsibility for PA decisions usually rests solely with the manager (see Chapter 4).

When these organizations espouse PA programs, such as mutual goal setting or another two-way communication technique, both managers and employees may sense discontinuity between the roles required for PA and the roles that characterize "business as usual." Although lower-level employees are typically responsible for the tactical aspects of their jobs, increased participation in goal setting, feedback or evaluation requires more involvement in the strategic aspects of individual performance planning. If this type of strategic involvement represents the only departure from a pervasive top-down approach, then PA may well be viewed as awkward and manipulative.

The degree of democracy, delegation, and openness implicitly required in effective, participative PA approaches may render PA meaningless in traditionally strong top-down organizations (McCall & DeVries, 1977). In contrast, collegial organizations that adopt PA programs emphasizing the manager's role as rater may create divisiveness and resentment as a result of the discontinuity between formal PA and informal, day-to-day working relationships.

Conflict with the nature of managerial work A study by Mintzberg (1973) demonstrated that the manager's job most often consists of brief, varied, and fragmented activities and that managers prefer current issues and nonroutine tasks. This study also characterized most of the managers' interactions as ad hoc rather than planned.

Traditional PA, in contrast, requires managers to engage in a process characterized by relatively long, intense, and concentrated activity focusing on past performance. When PA is a formal organizational procedure, it is usually highly structured and at least an annual routine. Further, PA typically requires planned, formal interactions with employees in which interruptions are discouraged.

Thus PA may well be in direct conflict with the nature of managers' preferences and work patterns (McCall & DeVries, 1977). This conflict may not be altogether unavoidable, but PA system designers should consider these issues when recommending forms and feedback procedures that require time investments. Alternatives such as shared responsibility for PA and more frequent, but less formal, interactions may help reduce this conflict by making PA fit more closely with day-to-day feedback. Also, the goals of PA programs can perhaps be scaled down.

Compliance with legal requirements The 1978 EEOC *Guidelines* provides a new set of criteria for PA effectiveness. PA, used as a basis for organizational decisions about employees, is treated as a selection device under the *Guidelines*. Validation procedures, reliability of ratings, consistency of policy applications, appeal procedures, and monitoring mechanisms used as indicators of compliance are becoming increasingly important in the implementation of PA systems. Perhaps most important, when a PA program is implemented in an organization currently engaged in litigation or with potential prima facie evidence of discrimination, PA can easily become the focus of legal controversy, restricting its flexibility and perhaps its usefulness in achieving some goals.

Administration of PA PA policies and procedures emanate from various sources—for example, from central corporate functions to individual line managers (see, e.g., Lazer & Wikstrom, 1977). The location of responsibility indicates the importance of the PA program to the organization and its willingness to commit resources to achieve the program's objectives. For example, if major responsibility for putting a PA program in place is assigned to a junior personnel staff member with no budget, the effort is less credible than one that is carried out by the vice-president of human resources. Human resource programs associated with top line-management functions tend to be perceived by employees as being important. In one unpublished study by the authors, the PA programs reported by employees as having highest priority and acceptance in the organization were those initiated by top managers in such line functions as marketing and engineering.

Programs administered at the corporate level in large organizations tend to emphasize administrative uses of PA. Whether the primary purpose of PA is officially administrative or not, corporate-level departments can more effectively deal with data collected for specific decisions than with the complexities of day-to-day performance improvement and development. PA programs with employee development as the primary purpose are better operated from posts closer to unit operations by individuals familiar with the business.

PA designers also confront the issue of resources available to apply to a PA program. Implementing a PA program can involve substantial amounts of both financial and human resources. As shown in Chapter 5, PA systems vary in terms of the amount of resources required and the time frame in which they must be expended (start-up v. maintenance investment). Also, issues such as whether the organization's personnel programs are facing close legal scrutiny may affect how resources can best be invested.

Relationship to other human resource programs If PA is to be effective, it should positively correlate with organizational rewards (Porter, Lawler, & Hackman, 1975). In fact, PA is often a stated basis for compensation, promotion, and career development decisions. A PA system should be functionally integrated with these other programs.

In reality, however, managers may not be able to use PA as the basis for rewards, because either too few rewards are available or there are so many rewards that all share them (McCall & DeVries, 1977). In high-growth situations, both relatively good and poor performers may get rewards. In recessionary periods when merit pools are decreased substantially, good performers sometimes suffer the consequences along with everyone else.

Even in organizations with a heavy emphasis on merit-based promotions and salary increases, little effort is often invested in PA programs. A "pay for performance" philosophy is only credible when a strong relationship is perceived between performance (appraisal) and merit increases (Lawler, 1971). In interviews with managers conducted by the authors, the "pay for performance" issue has emerged as a major source of conflict. Managers and other employees have reported that other factors mediate the relationship between pay and performance. Also, some managers have reported that they have "forced" some PA ratings to fit their salary decisions to either protect their subordinates or avoid conflict with them (Teel, 1980).

In contrast, some organizations treat other human resource programs (like salary administration and promotion systems) as totally separate from PA, often creating an aura of redundancy for PA or a sense that double performance standards exist within the organization. If a PA program is redundant with other programs or if its timing or format unnecessarily restricts its usefulness for other personnel decisions, it will be treated superficially or forced into inappropriate uses to preserve other programs.

Top-management support The lack of top-management support, loosely defined in the literature, represents one of the most frequently cited reasons for failure of PA systems (Beer et al., 1978; Haynes, 1978; Ivancevich, 1974). Since the term "top management" is often used to represent organizational systems, policies, and values, it is possible that "lack of top management support" is a construct which incorporates other factors previously cited, including these:

1 Failure to place major responsibilty for PA implementation where the program can be effectively carried out.
2 Failure to allocate resources necessary to implement PA (money, staff, time).
3 Failure to consider how PA must fit with other human resource programs.
4 Failure to identify a clear, organizational PA policy consistent with operating management philosophy.
5 Failure to include effective appraisal practices as one criterion in managerial reward structures.
6 Failure to actively monitor PA procedures and data for indicators of EEOC compliance.

Perhaps another factor contributing to a perceived lack of top-management support is the absence of a credible, visible sponsor for PA. A sponsor could be a key executive or a successful division that demonstrates the positive impact of doing PA well. Too often, key executives espouse the importance of PA for others and disregard it themselves. Active top-management support, defined in terms of both individual investment and integration of PA into the organizational mainstream, appears to be a necessary, but not sufficient, condition for effective PA implementation.

Determine Basic Design Parameters

In addition to examining givens and evaluating contextual factors, the decision about the purposes of a PA system is a central element of the design process. As discussed in Chapter 5, certain types of PA systems are better suited to administrative uses than to communication or career development. In fact, many organizations combine multiple PA approaches to achieve several outcomes (Teel, 1980).

The design of the PA measurement system and feedback procedures should flow from the primary purposes and context of the system. Development of the measurement system also depends on the positions to be covered and the performance criteria for these positions (McCall, 1978). Survey results show that formal job analyses are conducted in only about half of the organizations surveyed (Lazer & Wikstrom, 1977), although methods to ensure job relevance are becoming increasingly important.

It is also important to determine the parameters for the communication of expectations, observation, recording, and evaluation of performance, as well as the basic feedback and review processes. Once established, these parameters can be tested against the contextual information to assess legality and feasibility before elaborate procedures are fully developed.

Develop a Complete Design

Unlike Rome, PA programs have literally been "built in a day." Such programs have basically ignored all the design and contextual considerations discussed thus far. For minor changes in PA systems, the prior discussion may have limited relevance. In general, however, to increase the likelihood of successful PA implementation, the previous stepping stones to design probably need to be addressed in some form to make PA useful to the organization and its members.

The latter parts of the design process are those factors commonly considered to be the entire design task in many organizations. Developing a complete design involves tasks such as the following:

1. Drafting organizational PA policy.
2. Conducting job analyses.
3. Developing appropriate forms and worksheets.
4. Establishing monitoring procedures.
5. Making necessary links with other human resource programs at policy and procedural levels.
6. Assessing information and skills needed for training.
7. Testing out the measurement/feedback/training needs/monitoring loop to see if it fits together.

When these design tasks are viewed as only part of the larger implementation issue, more work is clearly required. The implication, not yet clear from the literature, is that such increased effort significantly improves PA effectiveness.

INSTALLATION: SOME STEPPING STONES

After the PA program has been designed, it must be introduced into the organization. Introducing a PA program typically becomes the responsibility of the organization's personnel staff. This can create some problems, because although personnel professionals may be best equipped to serve these functions, they typically have little credibility in the organization (see, e.g., Nystrom, 1977). Thus the perception of PA as "just another personnel program" is easily fostered among employees.

Recognizing this problem, some organizations have buffered their personnel staff by having respected line managers play critical roles in the introduction and training sessions. Sometimes line managers even conduct part of the training program. The purpose of these techniques is to relate PA to the factories and offices where employees spend their time.

Training Programs

A sound training program provides information such as the rationale behind the PA program, the policies and procedures to be followed in conducting PA, and an explanation of the terms used on the PA forms and accompanying materials. In practice, however, training sometimes does not occur. According to one survey, about 75% of the organizations surveyed provides some training on the use of the PA form (Lazer & Wikstrom, 1977), whereas another survey showed that fewer than 25% provides initial appraiser training (Locher & Teel, 1977).

But such steps, when taken, represent only a beginning in the training process. The fact that employees understand what they are to do is no assurance that they can, in fact, perform the tasks. Appraisal skills depend to some extent on the type of PA program selected (e.g., an MBO-type program requires skills in setting goals), but two general sets of skills are critical in PA: *(a)* performance measurement or rating skills and *(b)* feedback or communication skills.

There is a growing body of evidence that PA skills are developed most effectively through active or interactive training which often allows managers to practice evaluation and feedback techniques (see, e.g., DeCotiis & Petit, 1978; Haynes, 1978; Ivancevich, 1979; Spool, 1978; Warmke & Billings, 1979). By testing their skills during the training program, employees will have a more realistic idea of the problems and issues associated with performance measurement. Managers can practice feedback or communication skills through such methods as role plays or simulations. Rehearsing the performance discussion and confronting some of the problems in a training setting can make the PA interview more effective. And rater training has been shown by some to reduce psychometric errors (Bernardin, 1978; Latham, Wexley, & Pursell, 1975).

The movement toward more participative PA programs has raised the question of whether employees should be trained to receive PAs. There are several potential benefits of the more participative programs. First, such programs permit employees to participate more actively and more constructively in their own PA. Second, they provide an active, ongoing monitoring system for PA; the employee, having been informed of appropriate standards and expectations for his/her own appraisal, may be more likely to help maintain the quality of the PA process. Third, since many appraisees will eventually be managers responsible for appraising their own subordinates, the programs provide future managers with the information and skills to conduct appraisals. And most managers who give appraisals also receive appraisals from their own supervisors.

Training managers to give formal appraisals and day-to-day feedback is a widely accepted rule of thumb in introducing new PA programs, yet systematic PA training is still uncommon. This fact may explain why many PA systems fall short of meeting their goals. For example, Beer et al. (1978) found that MBO was the weak link in PMS at Corning and that further training was needed to increase the consistency of MBO use among managers.

Pilot Testing

A new PA program can be phased into an organization by first testing the program on a relatively small group of employees. In effect, a pilot test can be used to provide an initial assessment of the program and allows the bugs to be worked out before it undergoes more widespread implementation (see, e.g., Haynes, 1978; McCall, 1978). For example, one department of a relatively small organization or one division of a large conglomerate can be chosen for initial introduction and testing of a PA program. The employees are introduced to the program and trained and actually begin to use the system as part of their normal operations. The employees' activities are closely monitored, and modifications in the system are made as required. Once this step has been completed, the program is ready for wider dissemination in the organization.

The pilot site should be carefully chosen. It may be representative of the organization as a whole so that the results can be generalized to a larger number of employees. A strong effort should be made to select a site where the PA program has a good chance of making a positive contribution. The results of the pilot can serve not only a research function but also as an example to other units of the organization that PA can be used effectively.

Another way of phasing the PA program into an organization is to begin at the top level of management and work down through the lower levels. This method can be extremely effective, because top-level managers serve as role models and encourage their subordinates to carry PA further into the organization. Unfortunately, this method is rarely used, perhaps because executives often view PA as inappropriate at their level (see Beer et al.,

1978). Thus it is likely to be more difficult to phase the PA process in from the top than from a functional or geographic unit of the organization.

MAINTENANCE: SOME STEPPING STONES

Many PA programs have died on the vine because, after the initial introduction, there were no systems set up to keep the program going. Managers have returned to their jobs and heard nothing more about PA from the personnel department, their supervisors, or their employees. To help ensure that managers use the PA program on a continuing basis, the organization must provide some encouragement and ongoing support for PA programs (Haynes, 1978).

Some of the maintenance functions are best filled by the human resource and personnel staff who can follow up on PA training in a variety of ways. One typical way is to provide a reminder service to managers that involves sending out a notice to the supervisor (and sometimes to the employee as well) when an employee is due for an appraisal. Reminder systems are most appropriate in organizations where employees receive PA throughout the year (as in anniversary date systems). The use of reminder systems can encourage use of a PA program (see, e.g., Dwyer & Dimitroff, 1976; Ivancevich, 1974).

Human resource professionals can also provide continuing consultation to managers after training to advise and help them solve problems they have confronted in conducting PAs. This one-to-one, ongoing consulting can help managers who may not otherwise seek out the information they need, and it can help identify further training needs of the employees. Additional training programs could then be designed and offered, such as an annual "refresher" training program covering the total PA program or training in a particular component that had not been as thoroughly covered as necessary during the initial training session.

Support from line managers is needed to keep PA active. Encouraging subordinates to conduct appraisals or using a second-level review process (in which the supervisor's boss reviews and signs the completed appraisal) can help ensure that PA will be done. Ideally, managers convince their subordinates that appraising subordinates is an important part of their supervisory responsibilities. This can sometimes be done through informal methods; however, stronger, or more formal, ways of monitoring PA use can also be used. One method is to include appraisal of subordinates as a performance criterion itself in managerial performance appraisals; thus managers are evaluated not only on traditional business goals but also on how well they appraise their subordinates. Another method is to require a

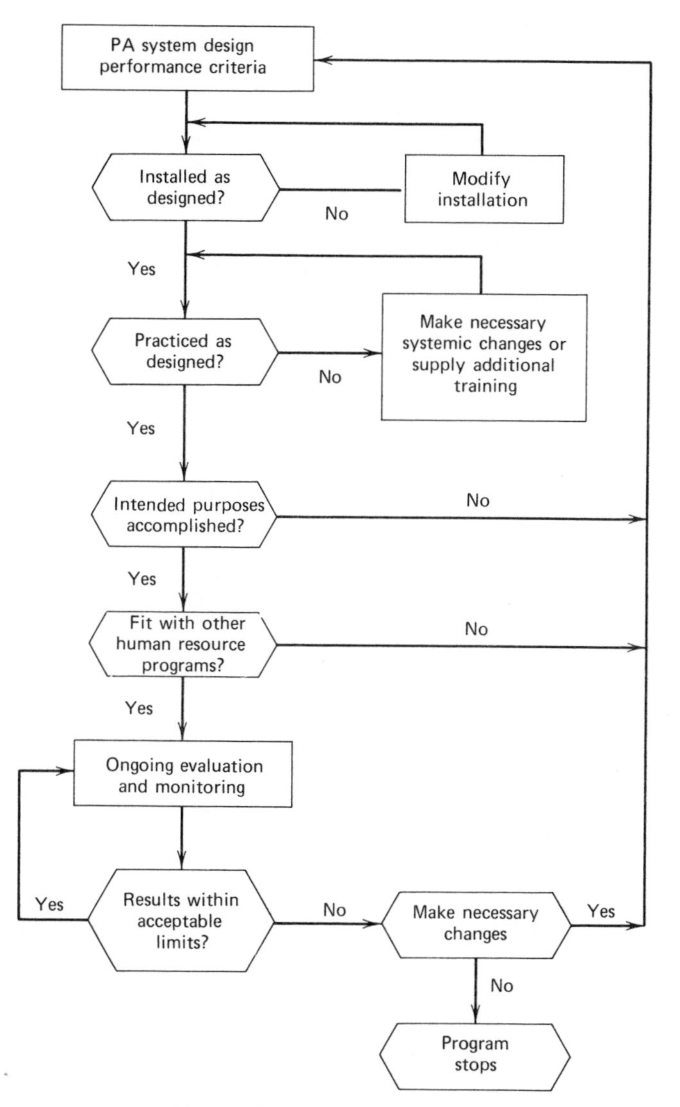

Figure 5 PA system evaluation.

recent PA for any salary recommendations to be implemented. For example, at Corning the Performance Development and Review (PD&R) part of PMS was required prior to submission of a salary action (Beer et al., 1978). This procedure is an enforcement device and also links PA with the compensation system.

Employees can also play an important maintenance function by periodically requesting either informal feedback or formal appraisal of their performance. If appraisees as well as appraisers have received PA training, more employees are likely to initiate PA, thereby creating a "bottom-up, top-down" support structure.

Maintenance functions are aimed at keeping PA active and visible in the organization. Different participants in the PA process play various roles. The important point is that the organization creates its own meaningful "check and balance" approach to actively track the PA process and keep employees at all levels aware of its importance.

Evaluation Evaluation of a PA program is a critical step that rarely occurs in the implementation process. From the stepping-stone approach presented, problems with a PA system and suggested changes could be determined by the answers to four basic questions:

1 Was the system introduced and installed as designed?
2 Are employees using the system as it was designed to be used?
3 Are the system's intended purposes and outcomes being accomplished?
4 Does the PA system fit within the organizational context, particularly in terms of other human resource programs?

Figure 5 shows the type of changes that can be made at points where the system does not meet its own expectations. As long as PA practices stay within the acceptable limits, no changes are necessary. An evaluation process does not have to meet the requirements of formal research to be considered functional. Incorporating simple information collection procedures into existing organizational systems can keep an organization in touch with the success of its PA system easily and with little additional effort.

IN CONCLUSION

The implementation process is a continuing one in organizations. The evolutionary cycle of PA recurs as the organization, work force, and environment change. The issues involved, however, remain the same. The PA program must fit the organization. The program's outcomes must be consistent with both the PA methods used and the business goals of the organization, and management must be committed to making PA work.

This chapter has explored some of the organizational factors influencing PA programs and has described some stepping stones to PA implementation. This discussion may well have created a monstrous spectre for PA not unlike that of a small craft, caught adrift in an ocean storm, expending total energy in just staying afloat, with no prospects of ever reaching shore. The reader at this point may wonder whether any of this is necessary or if PA requires more than it is worth.

The formal PA literature provides little guidance to those struggling with such issues. For organizations without the luxury of waiting for definitive strategies to emerge from the literature, there are two guidelines worth pursuing:

PA must be understandable to those who use it This applies to all types of PA systems, regardless of content, procedures, and purposes. Like all new systems, PA must be accurately explained and acceptable to those who are to use it.

PA must make sense in relation to other business systems Although effective PA is rarely a cure, the misuse of PA is often a symptom of disjointed applications of personnel policies, incentive and reward systems, reporting relationships, and so on. PA requires a well-defined, limited scope that contributes to the manager's job and the organization's operations.

In short, implementation of a PA program requires that employees have *(a)* at least one good reason to try PA, *(b)* adequate skills to use PA, and *(c)* a way to make PA an ongoing part of their jobs.

THE BOTTOM LINE

Doing versus prescribing The contacts we have with human resource specialists suggest that these professionals sometimes understand little about how their PA systems actually operate. Those who do have established strong links to the managers and professionals within the organization. These links can involve annual or biennial employee surveys in which questions are asked about both attitudes and practices regarding PA. Other specialists develop less formal ties, focusing on regular, informal conversations with both givers and receivers of PA. Only by reaching out to the PA constituents can you expect to get an accurate reading of PA as it actually happens in your organization.

Thinking before acting The mechanics of PA (such as the form) have an immediacy that often results in a total focus on them. PA forms and procedures should be established to achieve certain organizational goals. You must begin with a clear and finite statement of why PA is done in your organization, specifying how PA fits within your overall management system and why you think PA can improve the effectiveness of your organization and the people who comprise it.

Get to know the family The assignment of responsibility for human resource programs often results in fiefdoms around each program. One individual or group might have salary and compensation and another PA. Interactions among these staffs can quickly become embroiled in controversy, limiting the exploration of natural and functional relationships between these human resource programs. Minimally, a PA professional should get to know how the other human resource programs are conducted and received by the managerial constituents. Ideally, the PA specialist should foster ties with other programs that flow from the larger rationale created for PA.

The PA specialist is an organizational architect Remember that PA is an organizational system that you are trying to get placed into an often reluctant organization. Putting PA into use goes far beyond having an individual manager fill out a form on each subordinate. You should understand how other management systems have been installed successfully in your organization. If, for example, a new cost accounting system has been installed, do some detective work to find out how the system was designed, introduced, and implemented. Learning such lessons from your staff counterparts can give you insights about how new PA practices become an accepted part of your organizational architecture.

Participation is a good way to invest Employees can become very involved without handing over the entire appraisal process to the employee receiving the appraisal. Strategies such as joint goal setting are excellent ways of involving an employee. An employee can also be asked to help document how he/she is performing throughout the year. Participation can be created by assigning to the employee some of the record-keeping as well as the more substantive roles in PA. Such changes legitimize a more active role for the employee in PA.

7

Current Organizational Theory: Applied to PA Dilemmas

Item: In the literature, and even in the courts, PA systems are being asked to give an objective, accurate, and thorough picture of how an employee is performing. The reality is uncomfortably different. Appraisals are often cursory, based as much on whether the manager likes the employee as on what the employee does. Why is the ideal so elusive?

Item: Poor performers represent the group of employees for whom PA is particularly critical; it is the avenue for much needed improvement in performance. Yet these PA sessions often end up with the manager telling the employee to "try harder" and the employee reciting a litany of people and policies that make doing the job impossible. Why is this impasse reached so often?

Item: No matter how much priority your organization assigns to PA, you realize that managers will never give it top priority. Are there other ways of capturing an employee's performance that circumvent the manager? In particular, are there strategies for giving an employee a clear picture of how he/she stands on a wide range of skills and roles that would be useful in the current and future jobs?

Item: It is one thing to strengthen PA to a point where it gives reasonable input to administrative decisions. It is quite another to make it a potent tool for improving employee performance. Are there stronger techniques for making an employee want to and actually be able to change?

These four PA issues have three things in common: they are questions frequently asked by PA administrators; they are not obviously solved; and

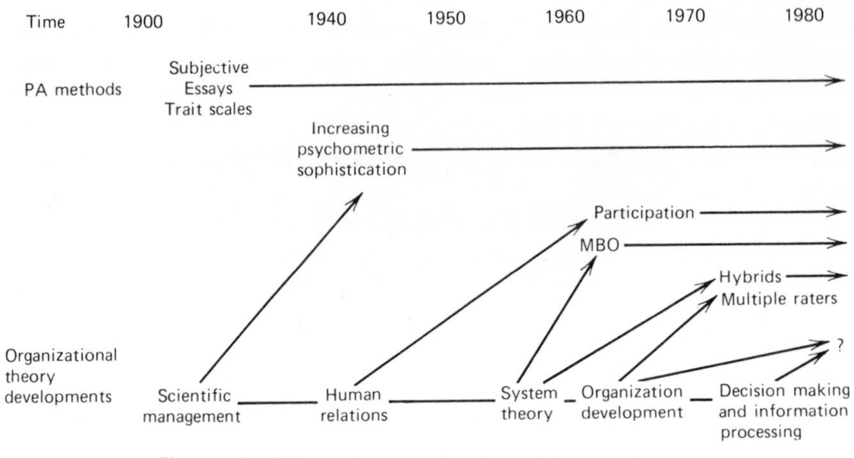

Figure 6 PA and organizational theory trends.

they are addressed in other organizational theory and development literature. The purpose of this chapter is to take each of these four PA issues and tie it to present developments in organizational theory to get a fresh perspective. This "wandering off" into other bodies of literature is not a capricious act. Rather, it reflects the belief we have that key PA developments are offshoots of larger organizational theory movements. This chapter begins with a historical analysis to prove that point and then moves to an analysis of each of the four issues.

THEORETICAL ANCESTORS OF PA

Major trends in organizational theory over the past 80 years are shown on a time graph in Figure 6, along with corresponding PA developments. The first major trend predominated from the turn of the century to World War II and is generally known by the term "scientific management." The emphasis of the trend was on the individual worker (the blue-collar worker in particular) and on the efficiency of the firm's internal operations.

The second major trend resulted from the Hawthorne studies of the early 1930s, conducted by Elliot Mayo and others, which concluded that the social aspects of organizations are at least as important as their technical aspects. This movement acquired the label "human relations" and is associated with such ideas as McGregor's "Theory Y" management. A third trend became evident with the advent of general systems theory in the 1960s which asserted that organizations had to be examined not only in terms of individual workers or groups but also in terms of workers' relationships to each other and to the larger organization and in terms of the organization's relationship with its environment. A fourth movement, organization development, crystallized in the late 1960s around several techniques and models for getting organizations and individuals in them to change. A fifth trend, initiated by Herbert Simon, James March, and others, has recently gained acceptance by many organizational theorists. This "decision-making and information-processing" approach to organizations emphasizes the inevitable constraints on optimal performance by individuals and organizations.

PA theory and practice have not been immune to these broader trends in organizational theory. However, the comparison of PA and organizational trends suggests that PA theory lags far behind general developments in organizational theory. And, as pointed out in Chapter 2, PA practice lags behind PA theory.

The increasing sophistication of PA theory and practice in the 1940s and 1950s grew from the early scientific management school's emphasis on the refined analysis of individual jobs, on performance, and on contingent reward systems. Scientific management was followed by the human relations school, but the latter's impact on PA was not felt for nearly 20 years until the proliferation of participative PA systems in the 1960s. These systems incorporated at least some of the elements of the human relations approach—in particular, the emphasis on collaboration between the manager and employee (McGregor, 1957). The introduction of systems theory in the 1950s provided the theoretical impetus for the MBO revolution in the 1960s and, more recently, for multiple raters (see Chapter 4), hybrid systems (Chapter 5), and contextual approaches to PA (Chapter 6). In short, PA practices have been predicted by larger trends in organizational theory that have preceded them by several decades.

ISSUE: OBJECTIVITY OR ELIMINATING "HUMAN ERROR"

Much of the PA literature is devoted to perfecting PA forms in the hope of eliminating error. However, based on evidence from the decision-making literature, we have concluded that PA errors are inevitable and reflect basic individual and organizational limits on objective evaluation of performance. These limits are of three types: individual "bounded rationality" constraints, the complexity and ambiguity of managerial jobs, and the role- and time-based constraints on the manager's ability to observe employee performance.

Simon (1957) first coined the term "bounded rationality" for the idea that, although people strive to be rational, they are limited in their ability to receive and process information about people and events. In Simon's words (1975, p. 198): "The capacity of the human mind for formulating and solving complex problems is very small compared with the size of the problems whose solution is required for objectively rational behavior in the real world." These inevitable limits on human information-processing capabilities formed the foundation for Simon's theory of why organizations and individuals rarely act as rational theories of organizations would prescribe. This theory is the first limit and helps explain why the ideal of totally objective PAs is illusory.

Bounded rationality would not be a problem in PA if managerial jobs and performance criteria were simple enough that complex information-processing skills were not required. However, neither is simple. The typical executive performs 19 to 32 different activities during the course of a day; lower-level managers may perform nearly 600 activities, with 300 to 450 discrete interpersonal contacts on the average during the same period (see McCall, Morrison, & Hannan, 1978). Evaluating that diverse set of activities is, even in an outcomes-oriented PA system, a staggering experience.

The complexity of the job is only part of the evaluation problem. The other part is defining performance in the job. Performance outcomes are often ambiguous, have long time lags, and send contradictory messages. For example, it may be years before it becomes clear whether a new product designed by a manager's team will be profitable. And even if the product does succeed, it may have taken the corporation into a new direction with little potential for long-term profitability. Together, the complexity of managerial jobs and the difficulty of identifying and assessing performance criteria constitute a second limit on objective evaluation of employee performance.

The third limit on PA accuracy stems from the role- and time-based constraints on observing employee performance (particularly if the employees are managers). Managers spend, on the average, less than 10% of their time with their supervisor. The majority of time is spent with their own employees and people outside their work group (McCall, Morrison, & Hannan, 1978). Clearly, a manager can observe only a small subset of the activities an employee performs. These activities are specific to the manager–employee pair and cannot necessarily be generalized to the employee's interactions with others. In short, the manager is involved with many individuals from both inside and outside the organization. Direct contact with an individual employee constitutes only a small part of the manager's job.

PA researchers have tended to view rating errors as a phenomenon peculiarly limited to appraisal. However, each of these constraints operates in realms of organizational life quite apart from the appraisal context. Random and systematic perceptual distortions of people, behavior, and events pervade organizations, thus precluding total objectivity in most managerial activities. Labovitz (1969) has noted that "organizations are not merely systems of related functions but also interpersonal social systems in which individuals are placed in close interaction with one another" (p. 194). Managers respond to each other on the basis of these interpersonal perceptions rather than on the basis of hypothetically objective behavior.

PA systems requiring rater evaluation (as opposed to those using only objective criteria such as attendance) inevitably tap into these subjective impressions. For this reason, a dilemma is encountered in designing and using PA systems. On the one hand, fairness to employees and validity in court demand objectivity in performance ratings. On the other hand, the reality of incomplete and biased information demands that subjectivity be a part of the appraisal process.

Steps can be taken to ease one from the dilemma of a need for objectivity and the reality of subjectivity. Some are listed here.

Avoid complicated forms Although this may strike the reader as a gratuitous comment that does not require a literature review to justify, the decision-making literature clearly supports this intuitive insight. Managers focus on salient, recent information about an employee (Slovic, Fischhoff, & Lichtenstein, 1977). PA forms that involve the manager's rating an employee on numerous items and dimensions serve only to confuse the manager and tax his/her patience; they do little to increase the accuracy of PA ratings.

Use other sources Each manager has only a partial view of the employee's performance that is biased by his/her particular position. Input from others in contact with the employee (peers, subordinates, clients, etc.) and the employee himself/herself act as useful cross-checks to the manager's impressions. Simple systems such as drop files that fit into the hectic pace of managerial work can also give the manager a powerful data base at the end of the year.

Tie into the subjective model Managers, and even organizations, have models of "what it takes to be effective" in the organization. These models often include traits and process dimensions of performance. For example, one executive's three-dimensional model for effective performance emphasized energy, intelligence, and integrity. Although such dimensions may not form the basis of a PA system, PA could be tied into them. The issue here is whether, through PA training and other means, the PA system can be linked to such intuitive models of effectiveness.

Confront the ignorance If one buys the notion that many managers have only limited contact with and knowledge of their subordinates, it may pay to inform the managers of that reality. If, in a PA training context, managers can be confronted with how little time they spend with any given subordinate, the manager might be open to working hard at getting a more complete picture of how an employee is performing. A first step in getting more accurate ratings is to get the manager to generate more systematic data on each employee.

ISSUE: ATTRIBUTING CAUSE

There has been a burgeoning literature in the past decade on how people make sense of others' behavior (Jones & Nisbett, 1971; Shaver, 1975). In particular, research in the area of attribution theory that is concerned with how individuals make attributions about the causes of their own and others' behavior has generated many findings relevant to PA. Some of the most important are cited next.

A phenomenon called the "fundamental attribution error" (Shaver, 1975) involves the tendency for observers to attribute the causes of an actor's behavior to the actor's personal disposition or traits, whereas the actor attributes the causes to external factors (e.g., the job or co-workers). The reason is that for the observer the behavior of the other person is the focus, and the environment is the central focus for the actor (Kelley, 1979).

Attributions of causation are moderated by various factors. One of the most striking is that people tend to claim responsibility for positive outcomes and deny responsibility for negative outcomes (Ross, 1977). (Parenthetically, this may be another example of the social sciences confirming the obvious.) If this bias holds for manager–employee pairs, the result is likely to be discrepant interpretations of both good and bad employee performance. When outcomes are positive, both the manager and the employee will take credit for it; conversely, when results are negative, both are likely to place the blame elsewhere, perhaps on the other person.

Another factor entering the attribution process is the perception of responsibility. As Green and Mitchell (1979) noted, it is possible to attribute an outcome (e.g., poor performance) to internal causes and yet have a person judged to be either responsible (e.g., drinking on the job) or not responsible (e.g., sickness in the family). The extent to which the rater believes the employee is responsible for his/her performance will affect not only ratings but also subsequent actions by the rater.

Attribution theory has seldom been directly applied to PA, but it is clear that managers are likely to gear their ratings to their attributions of causation and responsibility rather than to objective performance. Most PA measures involve judgments—not just describing performance but evaluating "good-bad" and "responsible for–not responsible for" dimensions. Some specific applications to PA are the following.

Source of conflict The tendency for raters to attribute causes of behaviors to the ratee's personal characteristics ("you don't have initiative") and ratees to cite external factors ("you didn't give me enough staff") is a source of conflict between managers and employees in PA. It could be useful to make both managers and employees aware of this universal phenomenon and to give them strategies for getting beyond this conflict. Simple role plays in which the manager assumes the role of a marginal performer defending his/her record can be useful aids in PA training. They often allow the manager to understand why the employee responds the way he/she does.

Focus on restructuring the task The typical response of managers to poor performers is to tell them to "work harder." Managers often assume that the employee is totally responsible for the outcomes. As Green and Mitchell (1979) suggested, an alternative strategy improving an employee's performance is to focus on external factors: Is the job properly designed? Is the employee being given adequate resources? Addressing these questions can provide clues, and solutions, to poor performance.

Implicit psychological theories Managers, like all humans, have rather refined theories of human behavior that color their evaluation of employees. For instance, when a person's achievement is seen as the result of considerable effort, the person's performance is generally evaluated more positively than when little effort is apparent in the achievement (Green & Mitchell, 1979). Thus PA ratings may confound performance with effort. Raters also carry their impressions from one performance dimension to another. Ratings of performance outcomes depend in part on how the rater perceives the employee's traits and behaviors. In general, a negative outcome (e.g., a decline in sales) is more likely to be attributed by the rater to external causes (e.g., an economic slump) if the rater perceives that the employee has relevant abilities (traits) and has put a lot of effort into the job. The same outcome is more likely to be blamed on the employee if the rater perceives a lack of either ability or effort, although the combination of low ability and high effort is viewed more favorably than the reverse combination of high ability and low effort.

Also, ratings on a performance dimension may be the product of inferences from other dimensions. For example, the rater may infer intangible characteristics like leadership or initiative from the more tangible evidence of whether an employee got the job done (i.e., from outcomes) (Kelley, 1979).

Attribution theory provides a remarkably well-delineated map of the mental gymnastics managers use when making performance judgments. This map can be very useful to PA designers and users to help ensure that performance components are not distorted so that interpretations of why an employee performed as he/she did are as accurate as possible.

ISSUE: ASSESSMENT ANALOGS

PA is an attempt by the organization to assess each year how an employee is performing on several important job-related dimensions. This assessment, as it is typically done, could stand considerable improvement, yet tinkering with some PA systems will likely yield only marginal improvements. There are assessment approaches in the organizational literature that would be useful analogs for PA. Both assessment centers and interpersonal simulations are coming to the fore in both the literature and in practice, and they deserve a closer look.

Assessment Centers

Can a set of tests and exercises be developed to create an overall picture of an individual's performance and predict subsequent success as a manager? This notion formed the basis of the first formal assessment center conducted in 1956 at AT&T (Bray, Campbell, & Grant, 1973). Since then assessment centers have been developed by and adapted to more than 1000 corporations (Finkle, 1976). As Finkle stated, an assessment center is "a group-oriented, standardized series of activities which provide a basis for judgments or predictions of behaviors believed or known to be relevant to work performed in an organizational setting" (1976, p. 861).

The characteristics of assessment centers are these:

1. Employees are assessed in groups (groups of 12 are most common).
2. Employees are assessed by groups, or teams, of trainers and managers.
3. Multiple tests and exercises are used for assessment, including objective tests (of knowledge, skills, and abilities), projective tests, interviewing, situational exercises (in small groups), and peer ratings.

Reviews of assessment centers (Bray, Campbell, & Grant, 1973; Finkle & Jones, 1970) indicate that the information collected about each participant is relevant to performance on both the individual's current and future jobs. The phenomenal success of assessment centers (Bender, 1973; Finkle, 1976) attests to the perceived validity of these ratings.

Interpersonal Simulations

As often noted, the managerial job plays itself out in an interpersonal setting. One element that is probably underrepresented in assessment centers is the interpersonal interaction required of managers. As Mintzberg (1973) noted, the interaction has Byzantine patterns, with clients, higher-level managers, suppliers, and peers all represented. Assessment centers do not fully test performance in that rich interpersonal context.

McCall and Lombardo (1979) reported the development of one simulation, Looking Glass, Inc. (LGI), that promises to be one of many simulations of the managerial world. LGI is a six-hour simulation of a glass manufacturing company. Participants are placed into 20 positions in LGI's three divisions and four management levels (from plant manager to president). LGI creates opportunities for both individuals and groups to grapple with problems ranging widely in significance and complexity. Preliminary evidence (McCall & Lombardo, 1979) indicates that LGI creates behavior in the simulation similar to that of managers back on the job. LGI does appear to accurately reflect the real work of managing, including the interpersonal activities that characterize managerial work.

Neither assessment centers nor interpersonal simulations were developed to be PA tools. Yet they seem to be sensitive indicators of how individuals do perform. What can we learn from these two recent developments?

Performance equals person and environment Both assessment centers and simulations recognize that to understand a person's performance you need to look at both the individual (experience, knowledge, etc.) and the environment (nature of the job, opportunities to take action, etc.). PA systems, in contrast, rarely go beyond the individual.

Neutral, trained staff A particular strength of assessment centers and simulations is the use of highly trained staff who have no particular relationship to participants. This combination of professional expertise and psychological distance allows the rater to give reasonably valid ratings of how each participant performs.

Standard stimulus Part of the value of the feedback that participants may receive after going through assessment centers and simulations comes from the strong normative data base. Trainers can compare the performance of an individual, or a group, on a standard task with a large number of an individual's peers. These comparative profiles can be valuable benchmarks for both the organization and the individual.

In short, these other techniques for assessing employees' performance have great potential. We are not proposing that such assessment tools replace PA but rather that these strategies for measuring performance and feeding information back to participants should be of more than idle interest to PA system designers. Although these techniques can be incorporated into PA systems to some extent, they can also be used to supplement formal PA programs; Chapter 8 points out why such supplementary programs are useful.

ISSUE: BEHAVIOR CHANGE

Even in informal chats with managers about PA, a frequent theme raised is the impotence of appraisal in creating meaningful change in an employee's performance. Managers often point out the infrequency of the event and the "handling with kid gloves" nature of PA, with both features seen as softening any possible impact.

One literature dealing with behavior change that has blossomed over the past decade is the area of organizational development (OD). OD is a collection of methods and models for creating change in people within an organization as well as in an organization's technology, operations, and structures (Friedlander & Brown, 1974). As Beer (1976) stated, OD techniques "constitute a growing social technology for intervening in, changing, and developing organizations" (p. 938).

The techniques used in OD efforts include laboratory training (e.g., T-groups or sensitivity training), diagnostic interventions (e.g., survey feedback), process interventions (e.g., team building and temporary task forces), and actual design interventions (e.g., shifting from a functional to a matrix structure). The field is remarkably diverse and growing in new directions. OD efforts do have some common models of change. For example, Schein's (1961) model states that organizations and individuals will develop if the following three events occur:

1 Unfreezing: shake up existing beliefs or behaviors.
2 Changing: establish new beliefs or behaviors.

3 Refreezing: stabilize new beliefs or behaviors through change in policies, norms, or organizational structure.

The effectiveness of OD in creating behavior change has been examined. Early reviews of the OD literature (e.g., Campbell & Dunnette, 1968) were less than supportive. However, recent reviews (e.g., Alderfer, 1977) reflect a continuing accumulation of successful applications of OD techniques.

Assuming that OD has created change in both individual employees and at the organizational level, the lessons to be learned for PA include the following.

Support for change OD interventions assume that an employee's behavior is not random; rather, it is probably the result of some consistent factors in the environment. As reflected in the original work at the Hawthorne plant of Western Electric (Mayo, 1933), a poor-performing employee may well be responding to strong forces in the environment (e.g., peer pressure). To get the employee to change, these forces (e.g., peer norms) must be changed. Because of this assumption, OD feedback is typically given to individuals in a group setting, with an emphasis on group problem solving. Through such strategies, group norms can often be altered to foster, not sabotage, change. PA systems seldom, if ever, use the power of the peer group.

The person or the job PA models typically assume the job is a given. The role of PA is to look at how the individual incumbent can become more effective in that job. OD efforts often take a broader look. Work with hourly employees in particular supports that a fair number of jobs have been designed in a way that creates boredom and even an inability to complete the task (because of insufficient resources) (*Work in America,* 1973). Through avenues such as job enlargement and enrichment, OD practitioners give PA designers a valuable lesson: don't take for granted the position and its location in the organization.

Role of the organization in refreezing The often-repeated saga of new PA systems being introduced into an organization, creating little impact on actual PA practices of managers, followed by the introduction of another system is an issue OD practitioners have addressed in a larger context. OD has developed several strategies to alter norms, policies, and even organizational structures in ways that support rather than undermine intended changes in behavior. PA practitioners could benefit by reading various OD case studies about how more permanent change was fostered (for an introduction, see Beer, 1976).

IN CONCLUSION

This chapter has purposely wandered away from the traditional PA literature to confront other basic issues and models of how individuals operate in organizations. It did so because a look at the history of PA practices reveals a 10 to 20 year time lag between the introduction of new organizational theory and the actual impact on PA practices. Current organizational theories reviewed were the decision-making model of Simon that emphasizes the limited information any manager can acquire when rating an employee, and attribution theory that outlines how managers assign responsibility for their employees' performance. Two current sets of organizational methods—assessment centers and simulation and organizational development—were reviewed, with the goal of giving PA designers the stimulus for exploring some nontraditional means for measuring performance and sharing those measurements with the employee in the most constructive way possible.

THE BOTTOM LINE

A review of the four areas covered in this chapter leaves one with a greater sense of the complexity of getting managers to conduct valid and useful appraisal of their employees. Many of the points in the chapter are detailed explanations of why things go wrong so often in PA (e.g., because of attribution processes, bounded rationality, or employee norms operating to keep performance down). Effective PA is a difficult organizational and interpersonal process that requires informed and skilled managers.

Designers of PA systems also should be well informed about relevant developments. Two suggestions are as follows.

Read organization theory literature This chapter was designed to point out several current themes in the large organizational behavior literature. Although the topics overlap only partially with PA, valuable lessons can be extracted. One gets the sense, for example, that some PA system failures could have been prevented if the designers had read a few OD case studies that focus on how to introduce a new management system so that the managers using it have a sense of ownership. Human resource professionals should become conversant with the theories behind techniques such as PA.

Find opportunities to depart from tradition Even as one reviews the PA literature the need for some fresh perspectives on the topic becomes obvious. Perhaps significant improvement of PA will require abandoning some long-held assumptions, such as the dominance of the supervisor in the process or defining major performance outcomes at the individual (as opposed to the team) level. Looking for PA analogs in other literature holds the promise of challenging traditional assumptions and molding PA to better fit the forces and realities it confronts.

8

Performance Appraisal in the 1980s

Corporations have never been larger or more powerful than they are today, but paradoxically, many corporations feel more threatened by external pressures than ever before.*

Predicting the future of PA is rather like going into a tailor shop to buy a suit for your brother-in-law who lives a thousand miles away and, oh, yes, is on a diet. Someone once said that the only thing certain about the future is that it is uncertain. Yet it is clear that we must look ahead to try to gauge the needs and pressures that will shape PA in the 1980s.

PA is one of many business systems in place within organizations. Issues raised in earlier chapters demonstrate that the organizational context is an important factor in designing and carrying out PA systems. There is also a larger context in which to examine PA which includes the characteristics and trends that surround organizations themselves.

The purpose of this chapter is to determine what effect these external factors will have on PA and provide some insight into how organizations might structure PA systems to have meaning in this larger environment and, indeed, contribute to their prosperity.

It has become increasingly apparent in recent years that businesses do not operate in a vacuum, insulated from community and government. Organizations and the systems within them are dramatically affected by environmental factors such as economic conditions, federal legislation, technological advances, and cultural trends. Examining these factors, we have found ourselves pushed outside the traditional organizational literature into a broader and less definitive set of resource materials. Since these readings typically do not focus on PA we have extrapolated from facts and educated opinions about the future some implications specific to PA.

MAJOR TRENDS

The beginning of a decade brings with it a barrage of predictions and

*Rona Klingenberg, "Institutions, Decisions and Social Change," *TAP,* 1979, **18,** p. 13.

projections about what will happen to whom and when and why such will happen. It is impossible to predict some major upheavals (e.g., wars and effects of political maneuvers); however, many of the influences are already present that will shape the future. The articles and books appearing over the past few years which attempt to forecast the future largely focus on three trends that have significance for business in general: increased government regulation, a faltering economic climate, and the changing labor market (see American Council of Life Insurance, 1979a; "Capitalizing on Social Change," 1979; "Challenges of the '80s," 1979; Otten, 1980; Raskin, 1979; Wilson, 1980).

Government will continue to play an increasing role in regulating the policies and operations of business. Although the primary target of government intervention has typically been big business (antipollution controls, antitrust litigation, antidiscrimination cases, etc.), the hand of government also reaches into small and nonprofit organizations. Many executives are recognizing a need to carefully monitor and influence the happenings in government and, in some cases, to modify their plans and activities to conform with current or expected action (Cody, 1979; Drucker, 1980; Segev, 1979; Wilson, 1980).

> The genius of the U.S. Constitution will be extended more and more into the workplace. . . . This pressure will require personnel policies and procedures with due process built into them at every step. (Odiorne, 1979, p. 27)

Growth in annual U.S. productivity has been declining and may continue to decline in the years ahead. Current and projected economic conditions have also received a great deal of press. The reasons for declining productivity improvement include not only the cost of complying with government regulations but also a reduced rate of investment in new producing capital and equipment, decreased research and development expenditures, the transition to a service economy (the "postindustrial society"), and a changing work force. Stagflation and OPEC further cloud the rosy glasses worn by many businesses in the go-go decade of the 1960s (see, e.g., American Council of Life Insurance, 1979a; Bowen, 1979; Ranftl, 1979). The ability of organizations to provide employees with financial incentives and rewards continues to erode. Moreover, many employees' jobs are likely to change as businesses identify and move toward more productive ways of operating and even ways to remain viable.

The demographics and values of the work force are changing. The tremendous impact of a changing labor force has been the subject of numerous recent publications and is, perhaps, the area that holds the strongest implications for the future of human resource systems. Whereas the total growth of the labor force will halve in the decades ahead (Wilson, 1978), increases in the prime, 25- to 44-year-old work force will be roughly double the average, and the level of women's participation will continue to increase in the early 1980s (Wilson, 1980). This new work force will be characterized by greater affluence, rising levels of education, a more probing and questioning attitude toward authority, greater institutional accountability, and individual self-actualization. The changing set of employees' values and expectations conflicts with many of the standard operating practices and systems used in organizations (see, e.g., American Council of Life Insurance, 1979a; Ford, 1979b; Howe & Mindell, 1979; Wilson, 1980; Yankelovich, 1979).

> Today's workers . . . want nothing less than 8 hours of meaningful, skillfully guided, personally satisfying work for 8 hours' pay. And that's not easy for most companies to provide. (Fritz, 1979, p. 35)

We attempt to identify the implications that these, and other, trends have for PA in the coming decade and beyond. This chapter examines what is happening and what is likely to happen to PA in light of these larger environmental factors and explores how PA can be tailored to best fit the most significant of these larger environmental issues.

HOW WILL PA BE DEFINED IN THE 1980s?

If a roving reporter were to wander down organization halls to interview people about PA, a common response would be this: "Performance appraisal? Oh, that's when my boss and I get together once a year to talk about the form that will be sent to Personnel." We have found that PA tends to be viewed as an annual, formally documented event. Even when a program such as MBO is used which involves multiple steps throughout the year and components that are broader than simply the evaluation of past performance, PA still connotes a once-a-year, fill-in-the-form type of activity.

We can find no compelling reason for this view of PA not to continue into the 1980s, with other ongoing or related programs seen as separate from PA. That is, programs that are designed as components of a broad PA system or are closely tied to a PA program will continue to be viewed as different from PA itself or as supplements to the PA process. Such programs include the goal-setting process, interim performance review, career-planning programs, training programs, job enrichment programs, and informal feedback on the job (Ranftl, 1979; Rosow, 1979; Yankelovich, 1979). The fact that

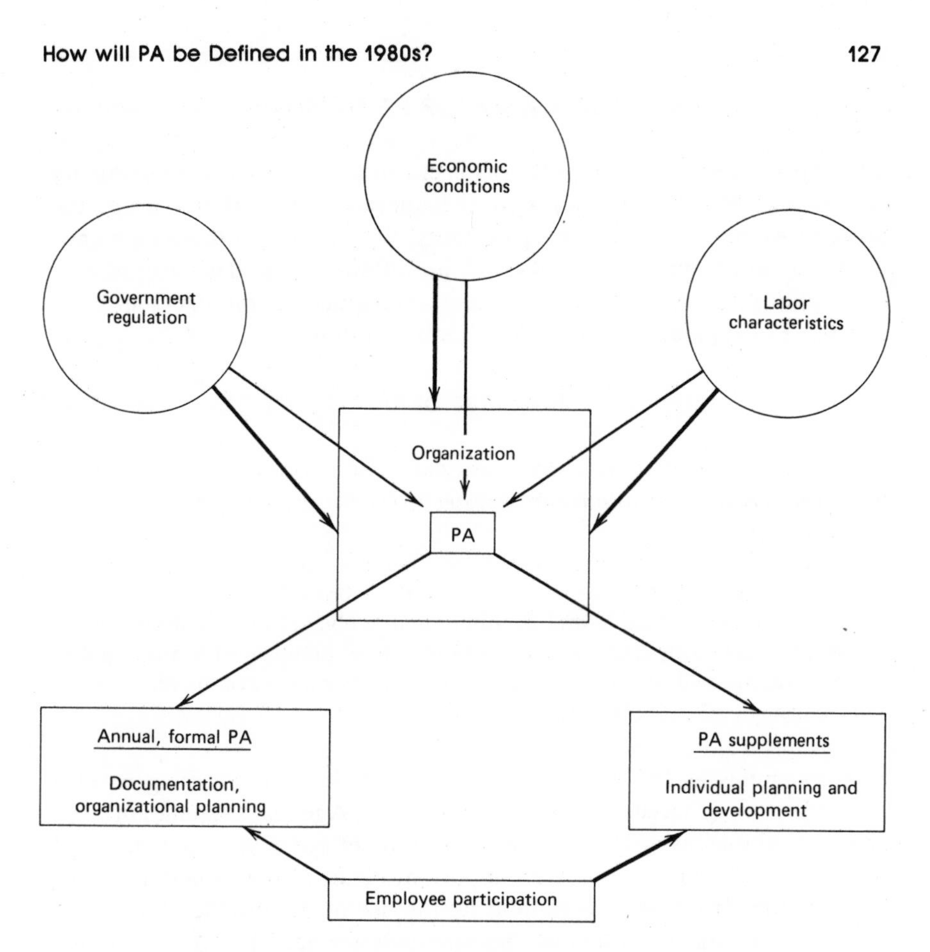

Figure 7 The impact of modern forces on PA.

such a distinction can be made between PA itself and related, supplementary programs suggests that they have different characteristics, serve different functions, and are carried out differently.

Both PA as a specific formal event and its supplementary programs will be important in the 1980s but for different reasons. PA itself is a critical factor in organizations' attempts to meet government requirements, primarily around issues involving equal opportunity. Related programs, perhaps less formal, are becoming more and more critical to organizations in terms of meeting employees' expectations; the characteristics of the labor market mentioned earlier are particularly relevant here. Figure 7 depicts the view we have of the major forces operating on PA and how PA can be used to respond to these in the 1980s.

ANALYSIS OF MAJOR PA ELEMENTS

The impact of environmental factors is examined in terms of four primary elements of PA: the purposes of the appraisal, the criteria used, the procedures involved, and the participants. Within each of these elements, significant environmental trends are identified and explored in terms of their implications for PA. To make this analysis more meaningful, PA as an event and the PA supplements are addressed separately.

Purposes of PA

When PA is considered as a specific, annual event, its primary purpose will be the documentation of administrative decisions for legal protection.

> Legal processes will become more common in the workplace, and possibly more law school graduates . . . will appear in labor relations, arbitration, personnel administration and consumer and public affairs. To offset this, lay managers will become considerably more familiar with the legal characteristics of the due process system than they have in the past. (Odiorne, 1979, p. 27)

Such examples as the recent Supreme Court decision rejecting reverse discrimination charges at Kaiser and the Age Discrimination Act amendment increasing the mandatory retirement age to 70 imply that legal considerations continue to be an important factor in personnel decisions. Further, the EEOC is now supporting the use of the broader concept of "comparable worth" in lieu of "substantially similar" jobs in evaluating discrimination cases (Cody, 1979).

It is no wonder that The *Wall Street Journal* ("Uncle Sam," 1980) headlines: "Uncle Sam will pose the biggest problems for personnel chiefs in the 80s." In some cases, organizations find that they have provided ammunition to the plaintiffs through legally unacceptable PA forms and practices or inaccurate written evaluations. With PA records being brought into court to support discrimination claims, it is not surprising that more attention is being devoted to performance documentation.

The trend to hold businesses accountable for the impact of their actions on society continues to grow.

> Corporations are being urged to meet new social goals, including an expanded concept of fairness. . . . The emphasis on fairness also fuels the drive on equality of the sexes and extends to such issues as the redistribution of income. (Klingenberg, 1979, p. 15)

"Fairness" as it relates to decisions regarding salary, promotion, development opportunities, and dismissal is certainly a concern in the ranks of the work force. In the context of a tightening economy and a questioning, rights-conscious breed of workers, organizations can expect to be challenged on these decisions and the underlying processes by which these decisions are made. PA is, of course, one of the primary processes involved.

The theme of individual rights has made its way into recent literature on the future of the workplace. The sense of being entitled to a job "as a social right," the sense that one is entitled to a voice at work, and an attitude that jobs should offer more and more of the basic necessities of life besides direct income have led to the conclusion by some that the conflict over rights may increase (see, e.g., Kanter, 1978). Individual rights have also been defined to include fair procedure, participation, and employee privacy; and it has been proposed that the concept be expanded to include the right to control working conditions and the right to a voice in decisions (American Council of Life Insurance, 1979a). Although some of these concepts may be a long way from specific legislation, they are nonetheless a part of the context into which PA systems must eventually fit.

Steps are already being taken to respond to the issues of legality and fairness before they become politicized. Some organizations are putting more effort into designing PA forms that will meet legal guidelines and providing backup for the criteria used in appraisals through job evaluation studies identifying performance requirements. Existing PA systems can also, in some cases, be consolidated and simplified, particularly in large and highly decentralized corporations where many different PA systems are being used (Cody, 1979).

Finally, managers in an organization should develop a sensitivity to the political implications of their actions in the area of appraisal. They need to

> be aware of what are likely to be the issues of the immediate future; what are the interests and expectations of the primary actors (customers, employers, public, special interest groups) on these issues; and what are the prospects for any relevant legislative proposals. (Wilson, 1980, p. 47)

Because there are currently no specific "government approved" models for PA systems (agencies within the federal government are themselves struggling with the design of PA), this strategy of increasing managerial awareness may be the most effective, broad-based way of responding to the issue of increased government control in the 1980s.

A second important purpose of PA will be for human resource planning or the use of appraisal documents to assess the needs and availability of human resources to carry out the company's goals. Formal human resource management progams are becoming more critical for several reasons. First, the changing demographics of the labor force are sharply reducing the supply of new workers that will reach companies in the 1980s; whereas the supply of prime working-age employees will grow, companies will not be able to replace employees with new, young workers ("Challenges of the '80s," 1979; Guzzardi, 1979; Raskin, 1979; Rosow, 1979; Wilson, 1978).

Drucker (1979b) has cited the need for companies to undertake "redundancy planning"—retraining workers now in traditional and manufacturing jobs for new jobs. He noted that labor unions are already pressuring Congress to impose redundancy planning on industry and that new jobs that are identified or created need to be productive, knowledge-based positions which are more consistent with a service-oriented economy and the educational level of the work force. "No longer will it be appropriate (if it ever was) to refer to workers as 'hands'—an industrial era term. The post industrial employees will more accurately be categorized as 'brains' " (Wilson, 1978, p. 11).

Another aspect of human resource planning is highlighted by the increasing emphasis on corporate strategic planning. Organizations, faced with rapidly changing environmental and economic conditions, are increasingly attempting to develop long-range strategic plans (see, e.g., American Council of Life Insurance, 1979b; Klingenberg, 1979; Segev, 1979). If the trend toward more corporate planning takes hold, more attention will be focused on the human resource aspect: "A strategy without adequate staff support is like a transoceanic voyage to a small island by dead reckoning."* These three elements—the stagnant labor force supply, the shift from manufacturing to service, and the burgeoning of corporate strategic efforts—indicate that human resource planning will become more crucial to organizations. The use of PA documents to identify the strengths and weaknesses of employees and identify those who can be retrained or shifted to alternate positions will almost certainly be an integral part of these planning efforts (see, e.g., Drucker, 1979a; Odiorne, 1979; Rosow, 1979).

A third purpose of formal PA will be to meet the demands of the work force for participation in decisions that affect their own jobs and their own lives. Raskin (1979) pointed out: "Most important . . . will be the need to give workers the opportunity to participate in joint decision making with management, for failure to do this will not only continue to diminish productivity, but may even aggravate it" (p. 25).

The notion of codetermination, although concentrated in the professional and technical ranks, is becoming pervasive among the younger, better-edu-

*Bruce D. Henderson, Chairman, The Boston Consulting Group, Inc.

cated work force (Ford, 1979b; Raskin, 1979; Wilson, 1978); a 1977 Yankelovich poll showed that more than half of U.S. workers surveyed believe they have a right to share in decisions that affect their jobs (Wilson, 1978). To the extent that PA represents a formal decision-making process in organizations, workers will increasingly demand the right to take an active role. Thus, PA will afford management an opportunity to incorporate workers' input in personnel decisions.

However, there is increasing evidence that participation on an annual basis in decision making is not enough to satisfy the new work force. That is, employees will not remain satisfied by participating merely in their own performance evaluation. Supplemental programs will be needed as ongoing vehicles for employee participation and control. The emphasis must be on systems through which workers can participate in developing and managing their own jobs and on "customized feedback mechanisms on achievement" that will help employees maintain their "own balance sheet" (American Council of Life Insurance, 1979a; Yankelovich, 1979).

> The better educated worker has a different self-image, a stronger sense of self-respect, a wish to be treated more as an individual, much less tolerance for authoritarianism and organizational restraints, and a different (and higher) level of expectations of what he wants to put into a job and what he wants to get out of it. (Wilson, 1978, p. 9)

It is clear that organizations must find ways of meeting work-force demands for more control, more feedback, and more challenge in their jobs. Some of the supplemental programs currently used, such as goal setting and career planning, are vehicles for employees to take an expanded, ongoing role in determining their own fate in the organization.

> Organizations must now advance from general affirmation and enthusiasm about personal career development to greater precision. The concepts and goals of education and development programs must be more precise, more widely understood, reflected in formal policy statements and translated into institutional and personal practice. (Howe & Mindell, 1979, p. 52)

The challenge to organizations will be to develop new supplemental programs and to use these programs as an integral part of managing and to apply them according to the needs of individual employees.

Performance Criteria

Increased productivity is certain to be a goal of PA for many organizations in the years ahead. Yet Yankelovich (1979) has suggested that true productivity depends ultimately on intangibles such as "dedication, caring, and a sense of responsibility for giving real service."

The identification of performance criteria in the 1980s and beyond is perhaps the most complex issue in PA. As personnel continues to grow as a significant fixed cost in many organizations, there will be greater pressure to identify and reward good performers and to improve, transfer, or eliminate weak performers. However, appraising the performance of professional knowledge workers in the postindustrial society entails a greater degree of subjective judgment than in a manufacturing economy. And for many jobs, a different concept of performance will be needed and valued. Some performance measures will fall neatly into already-existing PA systems, but many will not.

Primarily because of legal pressure on business to document performance, formal PA will increasingly rely on ratings of skill areas or areas of *competence derived from some form of job analysis* to ensure that they are job relevant. Drucker (1980) asserted that "jobs are becoming a nexus of rights of a species of property" and, because of this, "hiring, firing, promotion and demotion must be subject to pre-established, objective, public criteria."

At the same time, however, job responsibilities, particularly for managers, are becoming more broadly defined. Starting at the top, we see that the role of the chief executive is becoming a quasi-public job and that qualitative performance criteria are being added daily to the traditional quantitative (or financial) measures of chief executives:

> He or she is expected to be comfortable with the public's insatiable demand for accountability on many fronts and is expected to be capable of handling touchy situations. . . . There is a new personal judgment initiative being increasingly expected of CEOs by boards and shareholders. (Ford, 1979a, p. 40)

Expanding job responsibilities are evident at other levels of the organization as well.

> Management responsibilities, perhaps more than others, will evolve as the nature of work changes. Traditional criteria for success—the ability to plan, organize and supervise—will be expanded to include such things as workers' needs, hopes and aspirations. (American Council of Life Insurance, 1979a, p. 6)

Supervisors will be expected to find ways to achieve compatibility between the goals of the organization and those of the employee. Doing so may be as much an art as it is a science, and intuitive judgment will be needed (Ford,

1979b). Employee counseling and development, largely through supplementary programs, will become an increasingly important measure of managerial success (see, e.g., Ford, 1979b; Ranftl, 1979; Wilson, 1980).

As organizational operations and needs become less distinct from those of their surroundings, the degree to which managers and professionals become involved in community activities or take on "social responsibilities" is also becoming a more important area in appraising performance. The ability to forecast significant economic, social, and political events that will impact the organization will also increase in importance for more employees within and outside the sales and marketing function.

Standardized criteria for professional and managerial jobs will not sufficiently cover performance evaluation of the emerging roles that these employees will be playing in the 1980s. *Formal PA ratings are likely to be supplemented with individualized objectives for which some demonstrable measure of success can be devised.* These customized criteria will help fill the gap between general skill areas and specific job responsibilities of individual employees. The growing popularity of hybrid PA programs (using both rating scales and objectives) suggests that the combination of these two sets of criteria better reflects the performance and the needs of employees.

But the issue of subjectivity still remains. Perhaps if it is treated as part of the solution it will become less of a problem. Several authors, in dealing with management styles for the 1980s, have suggested that managers will need to come out of their wood-paneled sanctuaries and practice "old-fashioned, people-to-people leadership" (Ford, 1979b). Since the criteria and standards by which many workers will judge themselves and their jobs are largely subjective, the issue of subjectivity in managerial judgment of employee performance may be less of a problem if managers come to understand the value orientation of this new breed.

> If we involve these people in our planning, if we respect them for their values and attitudes, if we get to know them as individuals, then . . . we will have greater productivity than less, and more harmony than acrimony. It could be a real Golden Age for management. (Ford, 1979b, p. 11)

Appraisal Procedures

The procedures to carry out formal PA and supplemental programs will be geared primarily to their purposes and the criteria used. *The PA form itself will increasingly incorporate a set of rating scales around the competency areas identified for particular jobs.* These rating scales can be used both for human resource planning and to give employees skill-related feedback to help satisfy their desire to know. In addition, an overall rating of performance will probably also appear, as it does now, on many PA forms. The overall rating, as well as the individual scale ratings, provides quantitative information that can be plugged into computerized systems for organizations to monitor their use of human resources and provide necessary statistics to report on affirmative action programs. There is even the possibility that technological inroads will soon spawn computer programs that will analyze PA ratings and correct for halo and other errors (Schick, 1980).

Thus the translation of performance information into quantitative data will be one of the primary characteristics of formal PA procedures. It may be necessary to provide managers with training in how to use the PA forms in a legally acceptable way, and, in general, there will probably be more emphasis on sensitizing managers to issues of fairness and due process, particularly as these relate to formal appraisal procedures and consequent decisions.

Goal-setting procedures of various sorts will increasingly form the core of supplementary programs. Although many goals will be handled informally, particularly those dealing with employees' personal aspirations, more formal programs in career advancement and job structuring will probably spring up. As typical salary increases of 7–12% become more meaningless in an era of double-digit inflation, new, individualized incentive and compensation packages will become increasingly popular to attract and retain qualified employees. This "cafeteria" method of job design, job enrichment, and compensation will require more frequent and intensive conversations between managers and their employees to maintain an adequate match between the individual employee and his or her job (Bailyn, 1979; Dunckel, Reed, & Wilson, 1970; Howe & Mindell, 1979; Raskin, 1979; Yankelovich, 1979).

Thus a critical ingredient in these supplemental programs is that the manager maintain frequent contact with each subordinate, not only in a review function but also to provide the kind of personalized feedback to which employees feel they are entitled. Ford (1979b) predicts that "managers will have to manage less by memo and more by personal persuasion." The role of the manager as an adviser and counselor, as opposed to simply a supervisor, will be very important in implementing these programs.

Participants

The primary participants in both the formal PA and supplementary programs will continue to be the manager and the employee, although increasing reliance will be placed on appraisal information from and about others. The manager will remain a principal in the annual PA, because the supervisor will continue to be the best single appraiser of performance available in many cases and because the perceived legitimacy of the supervisor's role in making administrative decisions will continue to some extent (especially as such decisions relate to budget issues).

The employee's role, however, will become more active, through initiation of appraisal procedures, preparation and documentation in advance of the interview, and active dialogue during the discussion. Employees' perceived need to participate more fully in the decision-making process is leading toward a more equal balance in the roles of the manager and employee in the PA process.

Greater involvement by the personnel specialist as an internal monitor to review PA forms and procedures for compliance with legal guidelines is already occurring and will probably continue in the 1980s. Although not primarily a direct contributor of appraisal information, the personnel officer will serve in more advisory capacities to ensure that information on the form and the process used do not violate EEOC guidelines.

Managers are also more likely to solicit appraisal information from "third parties"—others in the organization (the manager's peers, the employee's peers, etc.) as well as outside clients and customers. More employees are likely to be physically separated from their managers because of technological advances in communications and information processing that permit geographic dispersion and alternate working hours (Morse, 1979; Wilson, 1978). Managers, having less day-to-day contact and familiarity with their employees' work, will obtain data and opinions from those who can better describe and evaluate job performance. Sales force managers have long faced this problem, yet they generally have sales data available as one measure of performance. Evaluating the performance of a systems designer, or a consultant, or a scientist working off-site poses more difficult measurement issues. As more jobs become service oriented, knowledge based, and based on interpersonal relationships with customers, the subjectivity of the evaluation process will involve a greater number of "expert" opinions.

In looking at who will be appraised in the 1980s, some significant trends are beginning to surface. Because of the increase in dual-career families and project teams, it is becoming more difficult to evaluate an employee purely on the basis of his or her individual performance. The growing number of professional husband-wife "packages" has created a need to evaluate the contributions of both family members in assessing and rewarding the performance of one. And attempting to isolate the contributions of an individual team member may not only be fruitless, but it may also miss the mark in assessing dynamic project work (Gibson, 1979; Hayes, 1979;

Weber, 1979). Methods aimed at motivating, directing, and evaluating teams of employees will become more common as managers recognize the unique aspects of team performance.

Participation in supplementary programs will be dominated by the employee in soliciting feedback and advice from the manager, peers, subordinates, and others both within and outside the organization. Employees with more education, a stronger self-image, and a need to know about their effectiveness and their future will seek out information about themselves and their role in the organization from not only their manager but also others in a position to observe, assess, and guide their behavior.

An employee's peers will, in many cases, represent a credible source of feedback because of the frequent contacts and the interdependence among each other for accomplishing goals. Subordinates' perceptions and opinions may also be sought out more frequently by employees through informal mechanisms as well as survey feedback instruments (Morrison, McCall, & DeVries, 1978) because of their perspective on the employee's leadership roles. Feedback from fellow team members will also be critical in some cases, since peer pressure in a shared assignment can be a very powerful force.

Also, the closer integration of personal life-style and the working place will cause many employees to define "how well they are doing" in broader terms than job accomplishments; the employee's spouse will undoubtedly be a source of feedback, particularly in the case of dual-career marriages. In a dual-career situation, the male employee who previously delegated much of his family responsibility to his wife will need to consider job commitments, including overtime, travel, and relocation, in terms of the impact it will make on the home front as well as on his job. "By no other change, therefore, than labor force participation of his wife, a man's ability to meet traditional business requirements will be somewhat diminished" (Bailyn, 1979, p. 19). Women in the work force, with high standards regarding their careers, will likely also have high standards regarding their marriages and the upbringing of their children. Thus the family will be an important source of feedback for employees, and, although this feedback may not directly touch the formal PA system used within an organization, it will be directly relevant to the criteria by which employees judge themselves.

The point is that employees want and demand more information about themselves and will find ways of getting the information they want, whether it be through formal systems sponsored by the personnel office, or through discussions with the boss, or by creating informal relationships and networks that can serve this function. The challenge to organizations, and particularly to human resource departments, is to find ways of providing employees with the information they want and to reduce the gaps and distortions between sources of information, such as between formal PA and supplementary programs.

CONFLICTS AND AMBIGUITIES

It is evident that PA, in its broadest sense, will be expected to continue meeting multiple objectives. The objectives themselves are, of course, subject to change over time. The assessment we have made of major environmental factors could be wiped out entirely by a major recession or any number of potential international scenarios.

Issues particularly relevant to the future of PA include these: Will professional employees' unions proliferate in the 1980s, or are unions in general on the decline? Will an inflationary recession temper workers' expectations of their employers or simply postpone the inevitable? Will strategic planning "catch hold" over the next few years, or is it merely a temporary, superficial fad? These issues are currently being debated in the literature (see, e.g., American Council of Life Insurance, 1979ab; Bowen, 1979; Etzioni, 1979; Klingenberg, 1979), suggesting that their resolution and the consequent implications for PA are at best tentative.

But we must proceed in the face of these ambiguities and assume that at least some of the objectives assigned to PA will hold up. In this case, we see that PA is expected to meet not only multiple objectives but also conflicting objectives. Whereas we have emphasized that separate parts of PA—formal PA and supplemental programs—will be aimed at different primary objectives, some conflicts are sure to arise, because the two parts must be integrated to some extent:

1 Individual freedom in goal setting may be stifled by centralized planning efforts (or vice versa).
2 The costs of developing and evaluating knowledge workers may be prohibitive in an economy characterized by cost-price squeezes.
3 Data that could be used in technologically advanced systems may already be outdated.

Conflicts such as these will not disappear over the next decade, but recognizing their potential impact on PA, we are led to a three-phased approach to designing and carrying out PA programs in the 1980s.

Phase 1: Design the formal PA program to meet current and projected legal guidelines. Information needed for human resource planning can be built in to some degree, using valid rating scales, but formal PA cannot be expected to satisfy employees' need to participate.

Phase 2: Add in the "real" components of job responsibilities as they develop and change, using individualized, objective-based programs. Nonstandardizable job elements and newly recognized performance criteria can be brought into formal PA programs through objectives. Legal guidelines appear to be more flexible in this area, particularly when employees play a major role in determining the objectives.

Phase 3: Fit the job to employees' overall life-style expectations by working individually (and often informally) with them; use of supplementary programs is critical in this phase. More give and take between the manager and employee to identify and incorporate personal values into job-related objectives will respond to workers' needs and may reduce the likelihood of legal action in other phases of PA.

IN CONCLUSION

If we have learned nothing else from this review, we do know that PA has not and will not remain constant in a changing environment. Adapting PA to the current and projected context should reflect not only the technological advances in measurement approaches but also the economic and social developments that shape its purposes and uses. Although these developments cannot be precisely forecasted, evidence for some trends is overwhelming, and designing appraisal systems to fit these trends is becoming increasingly important for organizations to keep or gain a competitive edge.

The model presented in the foregoing outlines a way to conceptualize PA, to break PA into manageable parts and serve some critical purposes in the 1980s. This model will have to be "fleshed out" according to the particular needs and resources of any given organization. It requires hard work, but it will not be without reward. In the words of Mills (1979, p. 162):

> Some organizations will correctly identify the requirements for change which the future will impose. Others will not. By identifying those requirements and initiating the first stages of an analysis and their consequences for his or her corporation, a manager may help the organization to be one of those companies which masters, and is not mastered by, the 1980s.

THE BOTTOM LINE

High visibility of human resource As a human resource manager, you are promised a more demanding and a more visible role in the 1980s. This role requires a well-planned set of human resource programs for hiring, promoting, motivating, and even firing employees. PA programs will be only one part of this wider range of human resource programs. Creating and reinforcing viable PA programs will be important, yet an even more significant challenge will be your rationale for the larger human resource package and how specific programs such as PA relate to each other.

The 1980s—no time to settle in The next decade will confront those concerned or involved with PA with continued changes in who works in organizations and why they work and what they do. You would be well advised to develop "sensors" in the several client groups you serve and professional groups to which you belong. The ongoing PA surveys of management and professional employees mentioned in Chapter 6 will give you one way to anticipate, or at least respond quickly to, changes.

Managers on the firing line Although historically the manager-subordinate relationship has been one in which the manager could set the rules and which was characterized by some privacy, that is changing. Managers must realize that how they handle key decisions such as promotion and termination is of interest to several parties, including one or more federal regulatory agencies. You need to prepare and regularly reinforce managers in strategies for handling employees in ways that capitalize on the more complex needs they now bring to the job. Clearly, managerial development will need to move from a once-in-a-lifetime "laying down the rules" toward an annual updating and expanding of skills.

PA—deciding what it is and is not One theme we started this review with was the unrealistic number of responsibilities some organizations assign PA. Those responsibilities will be even greater in the 1980s. The challenge will be to build new programs around such themes as career development and job enrichment that have their own separate identity and are not assigned to the PA agenda. That agenda is already chock full of significant issues.

References

Alderfer, C. P. Organization development. *Annual Review of Psychology,* 1977, **28**, 197–223.

American Council of Life Insurance. The changing nature of work. *Trend Analysis Report,* TAP, 1979. (a)

American Council of Life Insurance. Institutions, decisions & social change. *Trend Analysis Program,* Summer 1979, TAP, 1979. (b)

American Psychological Association, American Educational Research Association, and National Council on Measurement in Education. *Standards for educational tests.* Washington, D.C.: American Psychological Association, 1974.

Arvey, R. D., & Hoyle, J. C. A Guttman approach to the development of behaviorally based rating scales for systems analysts and programmer/analysts. *Journal of Applied Psychology,* 1974, **59**, 61–68.

Bailyn, L. How much acceleration for career success? *Management Review,* January 1979, 19–23.

Baird, L. S. Self and superior ratings of performance: As related to self-esteem and satisfaction with supervision. *Academy of Management Journal,* 1977, **20**, 291–300.

Barrett, R. S. *Performance rating.* Chicago: Science Research Associates, 1966.

Beatty, R. W., Schneier, C. E., & Beatty, J. R. An empirical investigation of perceptions of ratee behavior frequency and ratee behavior change using behavioral expectation scales (BES). *Personnel Psychology,* 1977, **30**, 647–658.

Beer, M. The technology of organization development. In M. D. Dunnette (Ed.), *Handbook of industrial and organizational psychology.* New York: Rand McNally, 1976.

Beer, M., & Ruh, R. A. Employee growth through performance management. *Harvard Business Review,* 1976, **54**(4), 59–66.

Beer, M., Ruh, R., Dawson, J. A., McCaa, B. B., & Kavanagh, M. J. A performance management system: Research, design, introduction and evaluation. *Personnel Psychology,* 1978, **31**, 505–535.

Bell, R. R. Evaluating subordinates: How subjective are you? *S.A.M. Advanced Management Journal,* 1979, **44**(1), 36–44.

Bender, J. M. What is "typical" of assessment centers? *Personnel,* 1973, **50**(4), 50–57.

Bernardin, H. J. Behavioral expectation scales versus summated scales: A fairer comparison. *Journal of Applied Psychology,* 1977, **62**, 422–427.

Bernardin, H. J. Effects of rater training on leniency and halo errors in student ratings of instructors. *Journal of Applied Psychology,* 1978, **63**, 301–308.

Bernardin, H. J. Beatty, R. W., & Jensen, W. J., Jr. The new uniform guidelines on employee selection procedures in the context of university personnel decisions. *Personnel Psychology,* 1980, **33**, 301–316.

Bernardin, H. J., & Walter, C. S. Effects of rater training and diary-keeping on psychometric error in ratings. *Journal of Applied Psychology,* 1977, **62**, 64–69.

Bishop, R. C. The relationship between objective criteria and subjective judgments in performance appraisal. *Academy of Management Journal,* 1974, **17**, 558–563.

Blake, R. R., & Mouton, J. S. Power, people and performance reviews. *Advanced Management Journal,* 1961, **26**(3), 13–17.

Borman, W. C. Exploring upper limits of reliability and validity in job performance ratings. *Journal of Applied Psychology,* 1978, **63**, 135–144.

Borman, W. C. Format and training effects on rating accuracy and rater errors. *Journal of Applied Psychology,* 1979, **64**(2), 410–421.

Borman, W. C., & Vallon, W. R. A view of what can happen when behavioral expectation scales are developed in one setting and used in another. *Journal of Applied Psychology,* 1974, **59**, 197–201.

Bowen, W. The decade ahead: Not so bad if we do things right. *Fortune,* October 8, 1979, 82–85, 88, 92, 96, 98, 100, 104.

Brady, R. H. MBO goes to work in the public sector. *Harvard Business Review,* 1973, **51**(2), 65–74.

Bray, D. W., Campbell, R. J., & Grant, D. L. *The management recruit: Formative years in business.* New York: Wiley-Interscience, 1973.

Bureau of National Affairs. Management performance appraisal programs. *Personnel Policies Forum Survey,* **104**, 1974.

Burke, R. J., & Wilcox, D. S. Characteristics of effective employee performance reviews and development interviews. *Personnel Psychology,* 1969, **22**, 291–305.

Bush, G. W., & Stinson, J. W. A different use of performance appraisal: Evaluating the boss. *Management Review,* November 1980, 14–17.

Campbell, J. P., & Dunnette, M. D. Effectiveness of T-group experiences in managerial training and development. *Psychological Bulletin,* 1968, **70**, 73–103.

Campbell, J. P., Dunnette, M. D., Lawler, E. E., III, & Weick, K. E. *Managerial behavior, performance, and effectiveness.* New York: McGraw-Hill, 1970.

Capitalizing on social change. *Business Week,* October 29, 1979, 105–106.

Carroll, S. J., Jr., & Tosi, H. L., Jr. *Management by objectives: Applications and research.* New York: Macmillan, 1973.

Cascio, W. F., & Bernardin, H. J. Implications of performance appraisal litigation for personnel decisions. *Personnel Psychology,* in press.

Challenges of the '80s. *U. S. News & World Report,* October 15, 1979, 45–60, 65–80.

Cody, T. G. Comparable worth rules: Another weight to balance. *Management Review,* May 1979, 31.

Cornelius, E. T., III, Hakel, M. D., & Sackett, P. R. A methodological approach to job classification for performance appraisal purposes. *Personnel Psychology,* 1979, **32**, 283–297.

Crooks, L. A. (Ed.). An investigation of sources of bias in the prediction of job performance: A six-year study. *Proceedings of Invitational Conference on Testing Problems.* Princeton, N.J.: Educational Testing Service, 1972.

Cummings, L. L., & Schwab, D. P. *Performance in organizations: Determinants and appraisal.* Glenview, Ill.: Scott, Foresman, 1973.

Dahl, H. L., Jr. Measuring the human ROI. *Management Review,* January 1979, pp. 44–50.

Deci, E. L. *Intrinsic motivation.* New York: Plenum Press, 1975.

DeCotiis, T. A. An analysis of the external validity and applied relevance of three rating formats. *Organizational Behavior and Human Performance,* 1977, **19**, 247–266.

DeCotiis, T. & Petit, A. The performance appraisal process: A model and some testable propositions. *Academy of Management Review,* 1978, **3**, 635–646.

DeVries, D. L. *A road map for developing appraisal systems: Ensuring a roundtrip.* Paper presented at the Office of Personnel Management Symposium, Arlington, Va., August 2, 1979.

Division of Industrial-Organizational Psychology. *Principles for the validation and use of personnel selection procedures.* Dayton, Ohio: Division of Industrial-Organizational Psychology, American Psychological Association, 1975.

Doyle, A. C. *The hound of the Baskervilles.* New York: Dodd, Mead, 1968.

Drucker, P. F. *The practice of management.* New York: Harper, 1954.

Drucker, P. F. Coping with those extra burdens. *Wall Street Journal,* May 2, 1979, 22. (a)

Drucker, P. F. Planning for "redundant" workers. *Wall Street Journal,* September 25, 1979, 28. (b)

Drucker, P. F. The job as property right. *Wall Street Journal,* March 4, 1980, 24.

Dunckel, E. B., Reed, W. K., & Wilson, I. H. *The business environment of the seventies: A trend analysis for business planning.* New York: McGraw-Hill, 1970.

Dunnette, M. D., & Borman, W. C. Personnel selection and classification systems. *Annual Review of Psychology,* 1979, **30**, 477–525.

Dwyer, J. C., & Dimitroff, N. J. The bottoms up/tops down approach to performance appraisal. *Personnel Journal,* 1976, **55**, 349–353.

Eisenhower, D. D. *At ease: Stories I tell my friends.* Garden City, N.Y.: Doubleday, 1967.

Equal Employment Opportunity Commission. Uniform guidelines on employee selection procedures. *Federal Register,* 1978, **43**(166), 38290–38309.

Etzioni, A. In future. *Next,* March–April 1980, 20.

Feild, H. S., & Holley, W. H. Performance appraisal—an analysis of state-wide practices. *Public Personnel Management,* 1975, **7**, 145–150.

Feild, H. S., & Holley, W. H. Subordinates' characteristics, supervisors' ratings, and decisions to discuss appraisal results. *Academy of Management Journal,* 1977, **20**, 315–321.

Finkle, R. B. Managerial assessment centers. In. M. P. Dunnette (Ed.), *Handbook of industrial and organizational psychology.* Chicago: Rand McNally, 1976.

Finkle, R. B., & Jones, W. S. *Assessing corporate talent: A key to managerial manpower.* New York: Wiley-Interscience, 1970.

Fisher, C. D. Transmission of positive and negative feedback to subordinates: A laboratory investigation. *Journal of Applied Psychology,* 1979, **64**, 533–540.

Flanagan, J. C. The critical incident technique. *Psychological Bulletin,* 1954, **51**, 327–358.

Fletcher, C. A. Interview style and the effectiveness of appraisal. *Occupational Psychology,* 1973, **47**, 225–230.

Ford, T. M. Changing ground rules for the CEO. *S.A.M. Advanced Management Journal,* 1979, **44**(4), 39–43. (a)

Ford, T. M. Tomorrow's employee: The supervisor's greatest challenge. *Supervisory Management,* 1979, **24**(6), 9–11. (b)

Friedlander, F., & Brown, L. D. Organization development. *Annual Review of Psychology,* 1974, **25**, 313–341.

Fritz, S. New breed of workers. *U. S. News & World Report,* September 3, 1979, 35–38.

Gartland, T. C., & Tornow, W. W. *An integrated R&D program for enhancing managerial effectiveness at Control Data.* St. Paul, Minn.: Control Data Corporation, Personnel Research Rep. No. 100–77, February 1977.

George, C. S., Jr. *The history of management thought.* Englewood Cliffs, N.J.: Prentice-Hall, 1972.

Gibson, J. E. Performance evaluation of academic research. *Science,* 1979, **206**(4417), 407.

Goodale, J. G. Behaviorally-based rating scales: Toward an integrated approach to performance appraisal. In W. C. Hamner & F. L. Schmidt (Eds.), *Contemporary problems in personnel* (rev. ed.). Chicago, Ill.: St. Clair, 1977.

Gordon, L. V., & Medland, F. F. The cross-group stability of peer ratings of leadership potential. *Personnel Psychology,* 1965, **18**, 173–177.

Green, S. G., & Mitchell, T. R. Attributional processes of leaders in leader-member interactions. *Organizational Behavior and Human Performance,* 1979, **23**, 429–458.

Greene, C. N. The reciprocal nature of influence between leader and subordinate. *Journal of Applied Psychology,* 1975, **60**, 187–193.

Greller, M. M. Subordinate participation and reactions to the appraisal interview. *Journal of Applied Psychology,* 1975, **60**, 544–549.

Greller, M. M. The nature of subordinate participation in the appraisal interview. *Academy of Management Journal,* 1978, **21**, 646–658.

Greller, M. M., & Herold, D. M. Sources of feedback: A preliminary investigation. *Organizational Behavior and Human Performance,* 1975, **13**, 244–256.

In R. M. Guion (Chair), *Job relatedness and equal employment opportunity guidelines: Alternatives to empirical validity.* Symposium presented at the 83rd Annual Convention of the American Psychological Association, Chicago, 1975.

Guzzardi, W. Demography's good news for the eighties. *Fortune,* November 5, 1979, 92–106.

Hackman, J. R., & Oldham, G. R. Motivation through the design of work: Test of a theory. *Organizational Behavior and Human Performance,* 1976, **16**, 250–279.

Hamner, W. C., & Schmidt, F. L., (Eds). Contemporary problems in personnel (Rev. ed.). Chicago: St. Clair, 1977 (printed with permission).

Hall, D. T., & Lawler, E. E. Unused potential in research and development organizations. *Research Management,* 1969, **12**, 339–354.

Hay Associates. Accent on appraisal. *Management Memo No. 293,* 1976.

Hayes, J. L. Creativity and the group effort. *Management Review,* May 1979, 2–3.

Haynes, M. E. Developing an appraisal program (Part 1). *Personnel Journal,* 1978, **57**, 14–19.

Hemphill, J. K. *Dimensions of executive positions.* Res. Monograph No. 98, Bureau of Business Research, Ohio State University, 1960.

Heneman, H. G., III. Comparisons of self- and superior ratings of managerial performance. *Journal of Applied Psychology,* 1974, **59**, 638–642.

Hillery, J. M., & Wexley, K. N. Participation effects in appraisal interviews conducted in a training situation. *Journal of Applied Psychology,* 1974, **59**, 168–171.

Holley, W. H., Feild, H. S., & Barnett, N. J. Analyzing performance appraisal systems. *Personnel Journal,* 1976, **55**, 457–463.

Holzbach, R. L. Rater bias in performance ratings: Superior, self-, and peer ratings. *Journal of Applied Psychology,* 1978, **63**, 579–588.

Howe, R. J., & Mindell, M. G. Motivating the contemporary employee. *Management Review,* September 1979, 51–55.

Ilgen, D. R., Fisher, C. D., & Taylor, M. S. Consequences of individual feedback on behavior in organizations. *Journal of Applied Psychology,* 1979, **4**, 349–371.

Ivancevich, J. M. A longitudinal assessment of management by objectives. *Administrative Science Quarterly,* 1972, **17**, 126–138.

Ivancevich, J. M. Changes in performance in a management-by-objectives program. *Administrative Science Quarterly,* 1974, **19**, 563–574.

Ivancevich, J. M. A longitudinal study of the effects of rater training on psychometric errors in ratings. *Journal of Applied Psychology,* 1979, **64**, 502–508.

Ivancevich, J. M., Szilagyi, A. D., Jr., & Wallace, M. J., Jr. *Organizational behavior and performance.* Santa Monica, Calif.: Goodyear, 1977.

Jablin, F. M. Superior-subordinate communication: The state of the art. *Psychological Bulletin,* 1979, **86**, 1201–1222.

Jones, E. E., & Nisbett, R. E. *The actor and the observer: Divergent perceptions of the causes of behavior.* Morristown, N.J.: General Learning Press, 1971.

Kane, J. S., & Lawler, E. E., III. Methods of peer assessment. *Psychological Bulletin,* 1978, **85**, 555–586.

Kane, J. S., & Lawler, E. E., III. Performance appraisal effectiveness: Its assessment and determinants. *Research in Organizational Behavior,* 1979, **1**, 425–478.

Kanter, R. M. The changing shape of work: Psychosocial trends in America. *Current Issues in Higher Education,* 1978 National Conference Series, American Association of Higher Education, 1–8.

Kanter, R. M. Power failure in management circuits. *Harvard Business Review,* 1979, **54**(4), 65–75.

Kavanagh, M. J. The content issue in performance appraisal: A review. *Personnel Psychology,* 1971, **24**, 653–668.

Keeley, M. A contingency framework for performance evaluation. *Academy of Management Review,* 1978, **3**, 428–438.

Kelley, H. H. *Personal relationships: Their structures and processes.* Hillsdale, N.J.: Erlbaum, 1979.

Kirchner, W. K. Relationships between supervisory and subordinate ratings for technical personnel. *Journal of Industrial Psychology,* 1965, **3**, 57–60.

Kleiman, L. S., & Faley, R. H. Assessing content validity: Standards set by the court. *Personnel Psychology,* 1978, **31**, 701–713.

Klieger, W. A., & Mosel, J. N. The effect of opportunity to observe and rater status on the reliability of performance ratings. *Personnel Psychology,* 1953, **6**, 57–64.

Klingenberg, R. Decision making and the forces of change. *Management Review,* December 1979, 13–16.

Labovitz, G. H. In defense of subjective executive appraisal. *Academy of Management Journal,* 1969, **12**, 293–307.

Lacho, K. J., Stearns, G. K., & Villere, M. F. A study of employee appraisal systems of major cities in the United States. *Public Personnel Management,* 1979, **8**, 111–125.

Landy, F. J., & Farr, J. L. Performance rating. *Psychological Bulletin,* 1980, **87**(1), 72–107.

Landy, F. J., Farr, J. L., Saal, F. E., & Freytag, W. R. Behaviorally anchored scales for rating the performance of police officers. *Journal of Applied Psychology,* 1976, **61**, 750–758.

Landy, F. J., & Guion, R. M. Development of scales for the measurement of work motivation. *Organizational Behavior and Human Performance,* 1970, **5**, 93–103.

Latham, G. P., Mitchell, T. R., & Dossett, D. L. The importance of participative goal setting and anticipated rewards on goal difficulty and job performance. *Journal of Applied Psychology,* 1978, **63**, 163–171.

Latham, G. P., & Saari, L. M. Importance of supportive relationships in goal setting. *Journal of Applied Psychology,* 1979, **64**, 151–156.

Latham, G. P., Wexley, K. N., & Pursell, E. D. Training managers to minimize ratings errors in the observation of behavior. *Journal of Applied Psychology,* 1975, **60**, 550–555.

Latham, G. P., & Yukl, G. A. A review of research on the application of goal setting in organizations. *Academy of Management Journal,* 1975, **18**, 824–845.

Lawler, E. E., III. The multitrait-multirater approach to measuring managerial job performance. *Journal of Applied Psychology,* 1967, **51**, 369–380.

Lawler, E. E., III. *Pay and organizational effectiveness: A psychological view.* New York: McGraw-Hill, 1971.

Lazer, R. I. The discrimination danger in performance appraisal. *The Conference Board Record,* March 1976, 60–64.

Lazer, R. I., & Wikstrom, W. S. *Appraising managerial performance: Current practices and future directions* (Conference Board Rep. No. 723). New York: Conference Board, 1977.

Levinson, H. Management by whose objectives. *Harvard Business Review,* 1970, **48**(4), 125–134.

Levinson, H. Appraisal of *what* performance? *Harvard Business Review,* 1976, **54**(4), 30–32, 34, 36, 40, 44, 46, 160.

Levinson, H. Management by objectives: A critique. *Training and Development Journal,* 1972, **26**(4), 3–8.

Lewis, N. A., & Taylor, J. A. Anxiety and extreme response preferences. *Educational and Psychological Measurement,* 1955, **15**, 111–116.

Locher, A. H., & Teel, K. S. Performance appraisal—a survey of current practices. *Personnel Journal,* 1977, **56**, 245–247, 254.

Locke, E. A. Toward a theory of task motivation and incentives. *Organizational Behavior and Human Performance,* 1968, **3**, 157–189.

Lopez, F. M., Jr. *Evaluating employee performance.* Chicago, Public Personnel Association, 1968.

McCall, M. W., Jr. Design and implementation of appraisal systems. In D. DeVries, M. McCall, & S. Shullman, *Performance appraisal workshop: Briefing book.* Greensboro, N.C.: Center for Creative Leadership, 1978.

McCall, M. W., Jr., & DeVries, D. L. *Appraisal in context: Clashing with organizational realities* (Tech. Rep. No. 4). Greensboro, N.C.: Center for Creative Leadership, 1977.

McCall, M. W., Jr., & Lombardo, M. M. *Looking Glass, Inc.: The first three years.* Operational Manual, Vol. 8 (Tech. Rep. No. 13). Greensboro, N.C.: Center for Creative Leadership, 1979.

McCall, M. W., Jr., Morrison, A. M., & Hannan, R. L. *Studies of managerial work: Results and methods* (Tech. Rep. No. 9). Greensboro, N.C.: Center for Creative Leadership, 1978.

McConkie, M. L. A clarification of the goal setting and appraisal processes in MBO. *Academy of Management Review,* 1979, **4**, 29–40.

McCormick, E. J., Jeanneret, P. R., & Mecham, R. C. *The development and background of the*

Position Analysis Questionnaire (PAQ) (Rep. No. 5). Lafayette, Ind.: Purdue University, Occupational Research Center, June 1969.

McGregor, D. An uneasy look at performance appraisal. *Harvard Business Review,* 1957, **35**(3), 89–94.

Maier, N. R. F. *The appraisal interview: Objectives, methods, and skills.* London: Wiley, 1958.

Mayo, E. *The human problems of an industrial civilization.* New York: Macmillan, 1933.

Meyer, H. H. The annual performance review discussion—making it constructive. *Personnel Journal,* 1977, **56**, 508–511.

Meyer, H. H., Kay, E., & French, J. R. P., Jr. Split roles in performance appraisal. *Harvard Business Review,* 1965, **43**(1), 123–129.

Mills, D. Q. Human resources in the 1980s. *Harvard Business Review,* 1979, **57**(4), 154–162.

Miner, J. B. Management appraisal: A capsule review and current references. *Business Horizons,* 1968, **11**(5), 83–96.

Mintzberg, H. *The nature of managerial work.* New York: Harper & Row, 1973.

Mirvis, P. H., & Lawler, E. E., III. Measuring the financial impact of employee attitudes. *Journal of Applied Psychology,* 1977, **62**, 1–8.

Morrison, A. M., McCall, M. W., Jr., & DeVries, D. L. *Feedback to managers: A comprehensive review of twenty-four instruments* (Tech. Rep. No. 8). Greensboro, N.C.: Center for Creative Leadership, 1978.

Morse, G. E. Human relations management: Concerns for the future. *Management Review,* June 1979, 47–48.

Nemeroff, W. F., & Wexley, K. N. An exploration of the relationships between performance feedback interview characteristics and interview outcomes as perceived by managers and subordinates. *Journal of Occupational Psychology,* 1979, **52**, 25–34.

Norton, S. D., Balloun, J. L., & Konstantinovich, B. The soundness of supervisory ratings as predictors of managerial success. *Personnel Psychology,* 1980, **33**, 377–388.

Nystrom, P. C. Save MBO by disowning it! *Personnel Journal,* 1977, **56**, 391–393.

Odiorne, G. S. *Management by objectives: A system of managerial leadership.* Belmont, Calif.: Fearon Pitman, 1965.

Odiorne, G. S. How to succeed in MBO goal setting. *Personnel Journal,* 1978, **57**, 427–429, 451.

Odiorne, G. S. *MBO II: A system of managerial leadership for the 80s.* Belmont, Calif.: Fearon Pitman, 1979.

Odom, J. V. *Performance appraisal; Legal aspects* (Tech. Rep. No. 3). Greensboro, N.C.: Center for Creative Leadership, May 1977. (Revised by K. J. Edwards, March 1979).

Otten, A. L. Europe's troubled businessmen. *Wall Street Journal,* February 13, 1980, 22.

Parker, J. W., Taylor, E. K., Barrett, R. S., & Martens, L. Rating scale content: Relationship between supervisory- and self-ratings. *Personnel Psychology,* 1959, **12**, 49–63.

Patten, T. H., Jr. *Pay: Employee compensation and incentive plans.* New York: Free Press, 1977.

Patton, A. How to appraise executive performance. *Harvard Business Review,* 1960, **38**(1), 63–70.

Pfeffer, J., & Salancik, G. R. Determinants of supervisory behavior: A role set analysis. *Human Relations,* 1975, **28**, 139–154.

Porter, L. W., Lawler, E. E., III, & Hackman, J. R. *Behavior in organizations.* New York: McGraw-Hill, 1975.

Prien, E. P. *Job-analytic strategies and their implications for content validity.* Paper presented at the 83rd Annual Convention of the American Psychological Association, Chicago, 1975, Symposium entitled "Job Relatedness and Equal Employment Opportunity Guidelines: Alternatives to Empirical Validity."

Prien, E. P., & Liske, R. E. Assessments of higher level personnel: 3. Rating criteria: A comparative analysis of supervisor ratings and incumbent self-ratings of job performance. *Personnel Psychology,* 1962, **15**, 187–194.

Primoff, E. S. *Using a job-element study for developing tests.* Personnel Measurement Research and Development Center, Standards Division, Bureau of Policies and Standards, U.S. Civil Service Commission, Washington, D.C., 1972.

Ranftl, R. M. Guidelines to productive management. *Management Review,* November 1979, 49–54.

Raskin, A. H. Management challenges in the 21st century. *S.A.M. Advanced Management Journal,* Autumn 1979, 25–32.

Robertson, D. E. New directions in EEO guidelines. *Personnel Journal,* 1978, **57**, 360–363, 394.

Rosen, A. Performance appraisal interviewing evaluated by proximal observers. *Nursing Research,* 1967, **16**, 32–37.

Rosow, J. M. The coming management population explosion. *S.A.M. Advanced Management Journal,* 1979, **44**(4), 25–32.

Ross, L. The intuitive psychologist. Distortions in the arbitration process. In L. Berkowitz (Ed.), *Advances in experimental social psychology* (Vol. 10). New York: Academic Press, 1977.

Rothaus, P., Morton, R. B., & Hanson, P. J. Performance appraisal and psychological distance. *Journal of Applied Psychology,* 1965, **49**, 48–54.

Salancik, G. R. Commitment and the control of organizational behavior and belief. In B. M. Staw & G. R. Salancik (Eds.), *New directions in organizational behavior.* Chicago, Ill.: St. Clair, 1977.

Sanders, M. S., & Peay, J. M. *Employee performance evaluation and review: A summary of the literature.* RATR No. 282, Naval Ammunitions Depot, Crane, Ind., 1975.

Sassenrath, J. M. Theory and results on feedback and retention. *Journal of Educational Psychology,* 1975, **67**, 894–899.

Schein, E. H. Management development as a process of influence. *Industrial Management Review,* 1961, **2**, 59–77.

Schick, M. E. The "refined" performance evaluation monitoring system: Best of both worlds. *Personnel Journal,* 1980, **59**(1), 47–50.

Schneier, C. E. The influence of raters' cognitive characteristics on the reliability and validity of rating scales. *Proceedings of the 37th Annual Meeting of the Academy of Management,* 1977, 255–259. (a)

Schneier, C. E. Multiple rater groups and performance appraisal. *Public Personnel Management,* 1977, **6**, 13–20. (b)

Schneier, C. E. Operational utility and psychometric characteristics of behavioral expectation scales: A cognitive reinterpretation. *Journal of Applied Psychology,* 1977, **62**, 541–548. (c)

Schneier, C. E., & Beatty, R. W. The influence of role prescriptions on the performance appraisal process. *Academy of Management Journal,* 1978, **21**, 129–135.

Schneier, C. E., & Beatty, R. W. Integrating behaviorally-based and effectiveness-based methods. *Personnel Administrator,* July 1979, **24**(7), 65–76.

Schwab, D. P., & Heneman, H. G., III. Age stereotyping in performance appraisal. *Journal of Applied Psychology,* 1978, **63**, 573–578.

Schwab, D. P., Heneman, H. G., III, & DeCotiis, T. A. Behaviorally anchored rating scales: A review of the literature. *Personnel Psychology,* 1975, **28**, 549–562.

Segev, E. Analysis of the business environment. *Management Review,* August 1979, 58–61.

Shakman, R. J. & Roberts, R. C., Jr. An evaluation of management effectiveness. *University of Michigan Business Review,* 1977, **29**, 24–27.

Shaver, K. G. *An introduction to attribution processes.* Cambridge, Mass.: Winthrop, 1975.

Simon, H. A. *Models of man.* New York: Wiley, 1957.

Sloan, S., & Johnson, A. C. New context of personnel appraisal. *Harvard Business Review,* 1968, **46**(6), 14–16, 18, 20, 29–30, 194.

Slovic, P., Fischhoff, B., & Lichtenstein, S. Behavioral decision theory. *Annual Review of Psychology,* 1977, **28**, 1–39.

Smith, P. C. Behaviors, results and organizational effectiveness: The problem of criteria. In M. Dunnette (Ed.), *Handbook of industrial and organizational psychology.* Chicago, Ill.: Rand McNally, 1976.

Smith, P. C., & Kendall, L. M. Retranslation of expectations: An approach to the construction of unambiguous anchors for rating scales. *Journal of Applied Psychology,* 1963, **47**, 149–155.

Solem, A. R. Some supervisory problems in appraisal interviewing. *Personnel Administration,* 1960, **23**, 27–35.

Spool, M. D. Training programs for observers of behavior: A review. *Personnel Psychology,* 1978, **31**, 853–888.

Spriegel, W. Company practices in appraisal of managerial performance. *Personnel,* 1962, **39**(3), 77–83.

Steers, R. M., & Porter, L. W. The role of task-goal attributes in employee performance. *Psychological Bulletin,* 1974, **81**, 434–452.

Taylor, L. R. *Explorations of the utility of behaviorally based rating scales for performance evaluation and counseling.* Paper presented at the conference "Managerial Performance Feedback: Appraisal and Alternatives," Center for Creative Leadership, Greensboro, N. C., January 1976.

Teel, K. S. Performance appraisal: Current trends, persistent progress. *Personnel Journal,* 1980, **59**(4), 296–301, 316.

Thornton, G. C., III. The relationship between supervisor- and self-appraisals of executive performance. *Personnel Psychology,* 1968, **21**, 441–455.

Uncle Sam will pose the biggest problems for personnel chiefs, in the '80s. *Wall Street Journal,* February 12, 1980, 1.

Vance, R. J., Kuhnert, K. W., & Farr, J. L. Interview judgments: Using external criteria to compare behavioral and graphic scale ratings. *Organizational Behavior and Human Performance,* 1978, **22**, 279–294.

Vroman, H. W. Differentiating MBO-appraisal systems: A contingency view. *Journal of Business Research,* 1975, **3**, 53–60.

Warmke, D. L., & Billings, R. S. Comparison of training methods for improving the psychometric quality of experimental and administrative performance ratings. *Journal of Applied Psychology,* 1979, **64**, 124–131.

Weber, A. R. Spousal nepotism. *Wall Street Journal,* September 17, 1979, 24.

Wexley, K. N. Performance appraisal and feedback. In S. Kerr (Ed.), *Organizational behavior.* Columbus, Ohio: Grid, 1979.

Wexley, K. N., Singh, V. P., & Yukl, G. A. Subordinate participation in three types of appraisal interviews. *Journal of Applied Psychology,* 1973, **58**, 54–59.

Whisler, T. L. Appraisal as a management tool. In T. L. Whisler & S. F. Harper (Eds.), *Performance appraisal: Research and practice.* New York: Holt, Rinehart & Winston, 1962.

Wilson, I. H. The future of the world of work. *S.A.M. Advanced Management Journal,* 1978, **43**(4), 4–13.

Wilson, I. H. Management and the changing public view. *Administrative Management,* 1980, **41**(1), 44–47.

Work in America. Report of a special task force to the Secretary of Health, Education, and Welfare. Cambridge, Mass.: MIT Press, 1973.

Yankelovich, D. Yankelovich on today's workers: We need new motivational tools. *Industry Week,* August 6, 1979, 61–65, 68.

Zedeck, S., Imparato, N., Krausz, M., & Oleno, T. Development of behaviorally anchored rating scales as a function of organizational level. *Journal of Applied Psychology,* 1974, **59**, 249–252.

Author Index

Subject Index